Railroaded or Not?

Into Federal Prison for Alleging that Zionists Orchestrated 9/11 and More!

By Steven A. Swan

Was Steve Swan Railroaded into a 9-Year Federal Prison Sentence to Prevent Him from Continuing to Widely Allege that Zionists had Orchestrated the 9/11 Terrorist Attacks and More?

Railroaded or Not?
Into Federal Prison for Alleging that Zionists
Orchestrated 9/11 and More!

Copyright © 2016 Steven A. Swan

No part of this book may be reproduced or transmitted in any form, or by any means, electronic or mechanical, including photocopying, recording, or by any other information storage and retrieval system, without written permission from the author.

ISBN: 978-0-692-79071-7

The author can be contacted at
contact@RailroadedorNot.com.

TABLE OF CONTENTS

DEDICATION III

PREFACE IV

CHAPTER 1. INTRODUCTION 1

CHAPTER 2. IRWIN SCHIFF 6
    The I.R.S. Put Me Out of Business! 10
    I Began Disseminating Schiff's Information to Others 11

CHAPTER 3. MY RESPONSES TO 9/11 13

CHAPTER 4. TARGETED FOR CRIMINAL PROSECUTION! 101
    I Got an Attorney to Represent Me 103
    I Tried to Enlighten My Grand Jury 105
    I Got Indicted, Arrested, and Arraigned! 107
    Federal Criminal Defense Is a Racket! 109
    Preparing My Defense 110

CHAPTER 5. NOT TARGETED BECAUSE OF MY INCOME TAX ACTIVITIES 118
    I Increased Disseminating My Belief Regarding 9/11 161

CHAPTER 6. MY TRIAL 163
    Preparing for My Sentencing Hearing 170
    My Sentencing Hearing 171
    Blakely v. Washington 173
    Objection to the Presentence Report and Recommendation ... 174
    My Resentencing Hearing 174

CHAPTER 7. I BEGAN SERVING MY SENTENCE........176
My Appeal..178

CHAPTER 8. CONCLUSION 183
Evidence That I Was Targeted by the Justice Department..............184

Dedication

This book is dedicated to the following individuals: first, my late best friend--Don "Donca""The Weirdo" Chase. Donca introduced me to the fact that our world is controlled by wealthy individuals and groups (oligarchs) who are able to get away with their massive charade by controlling the majority of information that most people receive. These individuals learned long ago that the most effective way to accomplish that goal was to simply own and control the major news, information, and entertainment networks. By doing that, they could also control our elected "leaders."

I believe that for numerous decades now, our world has been comprised of two parallel universes! One universe is the way that life is portrayed by the controlled mainstream media outlets and by our co-opted public officials. The other universe is life the way that it really is.

I am also dedicating this book to the almost 3,000 individuals who were needlessly murdered in the terrorist attacks on the United States of America on September 11, 2001. I believe that they were murdered in order to further a particular group's agenda. Where I differ with the way that those attacks have been portrayed by the controlled mainstream media and by our elected "leaders" is the identity of the heinous, ruthless, callous group of individuals who I believe orchestrated those murders.

Preface

This is my story of how I believe I was targeted by powerful individuals and unfairly and illegally railroaded into a nine (9) year federal prison sentence after widely and vociferously alleging after the September 11, 2001 terrorist attacks against the United States information detrimental to certain Zionists.[1] That detrimental information included my belief that certain Zionists had orchestrated the September 11, 2001 terrorist attacks against the United States and blamed them on their enemies in the Middle East (Muslims and Arabs) with the pretext of duping the United States into greatly expanding its military presence there and waging war on the Zionists' enemies. I also widely disseminated subsequent to 9/11 other material which was highly detrimental to the Zionist's agenda.

In the early 1980s, I was introduced to a variety of alternative news media which detailed how a number of special interest groups had subverted the governance of many nations (including that of the United States) and were dictating how those nations were to conduct their way affairs so as to serve those groups' own self interests. (That information was directly contrary to the information being provided by the mainstream media [MSM]) One of those

---

1 I believe that there are two different meanings for the term "Zionism." The first one refers to the belief that Jews have a right to a homeland in the Middle Eastern region of the world where the official religion is Judaism. Currently that homeland is a country called Israel. The second meaning of "Zionism" is a belief held by certain Jews and their supporters that they have the right to take over the entire Middle East by either displacing or exterminating any and all non-Jews residing there. When I use the term "Zionist," I am referring to individuals who subscribe to the latter definition.

groups was known as "The Bilderberg Group." Another of those groups was comprised of wealthy and powerful Jews who owned and controlled most of the world's news and entertainment conglomerates. I followed that alternative news reporting for many years.

By the mid-1990s, I was angry that powerful special interests had subverted the form of government that our forefathers and foremothers fought and died to institute, but I never really did anything about it aside from writing letters-to-the-editor of my local newspaper. Then in 1995, I met a man who was running for the office of President of the United States as a candidate for the Libertarian Party nomination in the upcoming 1996 election. That man considered himself to be the leading authority on the history, constitutionality, and misimplementation of the federal income tax. His name was Irwin Schiff.

Schiff had determined that, contrary to popular belief, there was no law making the federal income tax mandatory because, if it were mandatory, it would be unconstitutional. He also determined that anyone could legally stop paying federal income taxes. Over the years he had convinced many thousands of Americans to do so. And most of them had not suffered any major negative repercussions from the I.R.S.

After I met Schiff, I bought his books and audiotaped updates to them and I studied them. Everything that he was espousing also made sense to me. So I too stopped paying my federal income taxes. For the previous few years, I had been busy attempting to build up my small real estate agency in Auburn, New Hampshire.

After I informed the I.R.S. that I did not believe that I owed federal income taxes and that I was no longer going to pay them, it did not take long for the I.R.S. to seize my bank accounts and inform my real estate clients not to pay me if I sold their properties for them. Rather, they were to forward my commission money to the I.R.S.

In hindsight, I probably should have capitulated to the I.R.S. and saved the real estate business that I had worked so hard to establish. However, I was so convinced that the Government was illegally imposing and collecting income taxes and that it was my patriotic duty to stand up to it that I decided to try to disseminate Schiff's revelations to as many other people as I could. I spent almost the next five years doing so (while earning very little money, I might add).

Then the September 11, 2001, the terrorist attacks against the United States occurred. At the time, the Zionists had been receiving a lot of negative press because of a number of actions in which they had been engaged, so my first thought was that they had orchestrated the attacks in order to deflect attention away from themselves. Then I realized that the Zionists (both those within the U.S. government and Israeli ones) had probably orchestrated the attacks and blamed them on their enemies in the Middle East in order to dupe the United States into invading some of the Zionist's enemies there and also greatly expanding its military presence there. No country benefited more than Israel from the U.S.' response to 9/11!

From September through December, I authored many emails, letters-to-the-editor, etc. as to my beliefs, as well as detailing other information which was extremely detrimental to the Zionists. I sent my emails to hundreds of media commentators, news reporters, news publications and outlets, radio talk show hosts, elected officials, etc. I was especially active at the end of December of 2001. Approximately ten days later, fifteen to 20 armed, I.R.S. Special Agents were at my home/office with a search warrant and a letter from the U.S. Attorney for the District of New Hampshire informing me that I was the target of a federal criminal investigation into violations of the internal revenue laws!

I was indicted in March of 2003 of eighteen (18) felony violations of the internal revenue laws! After a six-day trial in February of 2004, I was convicted on all counts! I was subsequently sentenced to nine (9) years in federal prison!

There is a tremendous amount of circumstantial evidence indicating that I was not targeted by the Justice Department because of of my income tax activities. That evidence includes the fact that I was the only one of Schiff's many thousands of followers to be prosecuted. Even Schiff was not targeted until a couple of years later. And he may only have been targeted because I complained so much about me being the only one of Schiff's followers targeted.

Rather, I believe that was prosecuted and convicted to prevent me from continuing to vociferously insinuate that Zionists had orchestrated and carried out 9/11, as well as to prevent me from further disseminating other derogatory information about them. I have delineated that evidence in this book! I will leave it up to you to decide whether or not you believe I am correct.

If anyone has any definitive factual evidence that I was deliberately targeted for criminal prosecution by U.S. Department of Justice officials because of what I widely disseminated about 9/11 and/or Israeli spying and Israeli criminal activity within the United States, please share it with me. I can be reached at contact@RailroadedorNot.com. Thank you.

Steven A. Swan

Chapter 1. Introduction

My name is Steve Swan and I was born and raised in a small, rural town in western Maine in the 1950s and 1960s. Back then, the mainstream "social engineers" encouraged people to rebel against authority of any kind (including our parents) and to practice hedonism as much as possible. We were encouraged to "Tune in, turn on, and drop out!" and that "If it feels good, do it! ", among other things. Unfortunately, I heeded some of those messages. So after I graduated from high school in 1970, I left home, let my hair grow long, began drinking a lot of beer and smoking a lot of pot, and chasing a lot of women! In short, I "partied hearty!"

Shortly after graduating from high school, I moved to Manchester, New Hampshire. I went there because a friend from my hometown attended New Hampshire College there (now Southern New Hampshire University). Since life in rural Maine was very slow, I was searching for better social and employment opportunities.

My friend was also friends with a lot of fraternity brothers at the Kappa Delta Phi fraternity. So I became friends with many of them, too. Even though I was not a student at New Hampshire College, I was roommates with many of them over the years and I partied with them a lot. It was almost like I was an honorary fraternity brother.

Over the years I held a number of different jobs in the Manchester area—working at a tannery, a home appliance distributor, a furniture factory, an electronics assembly plant, singing in a rock band, working at a roofing company, doing rough carpentry, doing finish carpentry, as a home re-modeler, as a small-time marijuana and cocaine dealer, as a real estate broker, etc.

In the late 1970s while frequenting one of the bars in Manchester, I met a concrete truck driver named Don Chase. (His nickname was "Donca.") During the course of his daily work, Donca experienced a lot of down time while waiting for the concrete workers to be ready for his load. So he used his time judiciously by reading a lot of magazines and newspapers. Many of those publications were mainstream ones, but others were not so mainstream. Donca learned a lot from those publications. In fact, he related so many things to his friends that none of us had ever heard of before that we began calling him "The Weirdo!" Luckily for me, he shared some of those publications with me.

One of the major ones was a weekly newspaper from Washington, DC entitled *The Spotlight*. *The Spotlight's* primary emphasis was exposing the inordinate amount of power and influence certain Jews have in the world with respect to wealth, commerce, politics, the news-information-entertainment industries, etc. Certain ones of them have a tremendous amount of power compared to their relatively miniscule population.

(In the United States, Jews comprise only 2-3% of the population. However, the past few chairmen of the Federal Reserve System [which determines the United States' monetary policy] have been Jews; the past few Secretaries of the Treasury have been Jews; back in the mid-1990s, the majority of the international news and entertainment conglomerates were headed by Jews; many of the leaders of the various businesses within those conglomerates were Jews; many of the employees of those businesses were Jews; etc. In addition, the most powerful foreign lobby within the United States is the American Israel Public Affairs Committee (AIPAC). At its annual meeting held in Washington, DC each year, a majority of the members of the United States Congress, members of the Executive Branch of the federal government, and many other powerful and influential Americans attempt to curry favor with AIPAC and its members.)

Many of the powerful Jews exposed by *The Spotlight* were also Zionists! (See my definition of "Zionism" at Footnote No. 1 of this book.)

Another major area of emphasis of *The Spotlight* was reporting upon another facet of the unelected ruling elite which controls much of our collective lives. That facet is the "Bilderberg Group." This group is comprised of the global leaders of commerce and industry, elected officials of many countries, royalty, military leaders, heads of labor unions, heads of news and entertainment industry companies, etc. Even though the heads of the global news and entertainment industries regularly attend the Bilderberg Group's annual meetings, nothing is ever reported about those meetings in the mainstream news media.

Thanks to my friend, Donca, I became a loyal subscriber of *The Spotlight* and I was able to follow the actions of these two groups. (A few years later, *The Spotlight* was put out of business by the "Powers-That-Be." It was succeeded by another weekly newspaper entitled the *American Free Press*, which is still in publication.)

I have noticed over the years that while these two groups are separate entities, there are many areas in which their interests overlap. For example, much of the world's news and entertainment industries are controlled by Zionists or those sympathetic to their wishes. However, not all of them attend the annual Bilderberg Group confab. But many of the leaders of the individual mediums do, *e.g.*, *The New York Times*, the *Washington Post*, *USA Today*, the individual radio and television networks, etc.

I am not certain if there are power struggles among the individual members of these two groups or if they tend to co-exist peacefully. What I do believe is that because of the usurpation of power and influence by members of the Bilderberg Group and by Zionists from our elected "leaders", our society as a whole has become totally corrupted!

In a continuing effort to try to discern the truth about what was really going on in the world, I also began following other patriotic, America-First, anti-New World Order, alternative media. I listened to many different radio talk-show hosts on AM radio such as Pat Buchanan, Lt. Col. James "Bo" Gritz, Chuck Harder, etc. (AM radio used to be an excellent venue for these patriots until the globalist[2], ruling-elite discovered how powerful a medium it was and installed talk-show hosts sympathetic to their own agenda, like Rush Limbaugh, etc. After the patriotic radio talk-show hosts were ousted from AM radio, many of them moved to shortwave radio and satellite. Then as the Internet came into its own, many of them moved there.)

Another patriotic American whose disseminations Donca introduced me to was Dr. William Pierce. Dr. Pierce was also concerned about the inordinate amount of global power and influence certain Zionists had acquired and how they were able to affect our collective lives. He formed an organization he called the *National Alliance* in order to try to counterbalance that power and influence. The *National Alliance* had a weekly newsletter, as well as a weekly Internet and radio podcast entitled *National Dissident Voices.* Unfortunately, Dr. Pierce suffered an untimely heart attack at home one day, from which he succumbed. Was it a natural heart attack or was it inflicted upon him? Only he and possibly others know for sure.

Many of us America-First, patriotic, Populist Americans had become extremely concerned about our perception that many of our Government officials were straying further and further away from the limiting principles of the U.S. Constitution and were instead doing whatever they wanted. Many patriots began organizing themselves into groups in order to disseminate information about their concerns. Some of these groups organized as militias, which according to the original U.S. Constitution, were composed of all able-bodied men between the ages of 18 and 45 years old.

On April 19, 1775, the first battles of the American Revolutionary War began in Lexington and Concord, Massachusetts. On its anniversary in 1993 under the Presidency of William Clinton, the U.S. Government

---

2   The term "globalist" refers to those wishing to create a global system of governance with themselves in complete control.

incinerated 76 individuals (including children) at their Branch Davidian religious compound in Waco, Texas. Many patriots believed that the Waco massacre was conducted by the Government to test the amount of outrage such an incident would cause among the American populace. This incident, in conjunction with another one in Ruby Ridge, Idaho a year earlier, led to a lot more anxiety among the militia groups about Government subversion of the U.S. Constitution and the rights of the American people.

On April 19, 1995 (two years after Waco), a massive bomb exploded at the Murrah Federal Building in Oklahoma City, Oklahoma, killing 186 people and injured 680 others! Timothy McVeigh and Terry Nichols were convicted of causing the blast. After McVeigh was identified as a militia movement sympathizer, the movement itself became more vilified by the mainstream media. However many individuals believe that the bombing was instead an inside operation perpetrated expressly for the purpose of vilifying militias and anyone else concerned about the usurpation of power by Government officials.

Throughout the 1980s and early 1990s, I read and listened to a lot of patriotic, America-First, anti-New World Order media and learned a lot of information that was more or less suppressed by the mainstream media. The more I learned about how corrupt our society and those in power had become, the angrier I got. I tried to disseminate what I had learned to others by writing many letters-to-the-editors of various newspapers, calling in to local radio talk shows, and attending many patriotic gatherings. However, I never really acted upon my anger.

Chapter 2. Irwin Schiff

Then in March of 1995, I heard a very energetic, very persuasive individual on a radio talk-show who considered himself to be America's leading authority on the history, constitutionality, and implementation of the federal income tax. I believe that he was approximately 68 years old at the time. He believed that the federal income tax was entirely voluntary and that no one was legally required to pay it! That man was Irwin Schiff.

Over the years Schiff had written a number of books on federal income taxes and he had done whatever he could think of to disseminate his information to others. In 1982, he wrote a book entitled *How Anyone Can Legally Stop Paying Income Taxes*. In 1985, he wrote *The Great Income Tax Hoax*."And in 1990, he wrote *The Federal Mafia: How It Illegally Imposes and Unlawfully Collects Income Taxes*. Over approximately a 15-year period, he had convinced hundreds of thousands of Americans that the payment of the federal income tax was entirely voluntary and that the government was imposing and collecting it illegally.

Schiff was originally from New Haven, Connecticut and was a graduate of the University of Connecticut. He earned a Bachelor of Science (B.S.) degree there with dual majors in accounting and economics.

In 1968, U.S. Senator John Tower of Texas was the chairman of the Senate Banking Committee. He asked Schiff to testify before the committee as an expert on money at a time when the Government was considering abandoning the use of gold and silver to back the value of the U.S. dollar. Tower asked Schiff to testify as a money expert based solely on a series of letters Schiff had written to him on the subject.

The reason that Schiff was being interviewed on the radio was to promote his latest book, *The Federal Mafia*. He believed that the federal income tax was the biggest fraud ever perpetrated upon the American people and that the Government was able to conceal that fact by making the

Internal Revenue Code as complex and indecipherable as possible.

After the Schiff interview was over, I ordered Schiff's book. However, I was so busy attempting to build up my fledgling small real estate agency that I never got around to reading it.

One of the interesting things about living in New Hampshire is that every four years the First-in-the-Nation Presidential Primary is held to begin the nomination process for the presidential candidates for the major political parties. And in addition to the well-known candidates appearing to campaign for votes, there are also all kinds of other groups and candidates present attempting to disseminate their respective messages.

Since the next New Hampshire Primary was to be held in the early part of 1996, many candidates were already campaigning in the Fall of 1995. One of them was Irwin Schiff. He had decided that an effective way to disseminate his belief that the federal income tax was the biggest fraud ever perpetrated upon the American people might be to campaign for the office of President of the United States.

Since Schiff was a strict Constitutionalist (one who believes that the U.S. Constitution means what it did when it was written rather than being malleable and able to change with the times) and a staunch believer in limited Government, he decided to campaign for the nomination of the Libertarian Party, which was quite active and popular in the 1990s.

On October 31, 1995, I read an article in the *New Hampshire Sunday News (Union Leader)*, stating that the New Hampshire Libertarian Party was holding it annual convention that day in the State capitol of Concord. The article also stated that Schiff was going to be the luncheon speaker and that anyone could attend his speech. So I decided to attend and listen to the man I had heard being interviewed on the radio a few months earlier and whose book I had purchased but never read.

I attended Schiff's speech which primarily consisted of him explaining that if he were elected President, he would expose the fraud of the federal income tax so that everyone would know that it was a voluntary tax and he would also disband the Internal Revenue Service. Since many of the attendees were already familiar with Schiff's positions, his speech was well-received.

After the luncheon (while the rest of the Libertarians continued with their convention), I and three other people sat speaking with Schiff in the hotel lobby for the next three-four hours! Schiff was an extremely dynamic and persuasive speaker and we sat there fascinated as he disseminated his beliefs and recounted many facets of himself to us. I then decided that I was going to read *The Federal Mafia*. I also purchased from him some audio-taped updates to his book.

I also learned that Schiff's headquarters were a highly-visible office on "The Strip" in Las Vegas, Nevada. From there he sold his books and audiotape updates to them. He also acted as a consultant to those wishing to use his discoveries to stop the government from illegally imposing and collecting their taxes. In addition, Schiff also had his own 2- to 3-hour nightly radio show on AM, shortwave, and satellite radio in which he disseminated his information. (The length of his show varied from time to time.) He had also been interviewed many times on national and local TV programs, radio programs, newspapers, magazines, etc.

So I read *The Federal Mafia* and listened to the audio-taped updates to it. I also began listening to Schiff's radio program every week night. In it, he discussed the latest information that he had learned relative to federal income taxes and related the latest interactions that had occurred between him or his followers and the I.R.S. (Schiff did not spend all of his radio time talking about income taxes, though. He began almost every program with a discussion of the current economic situation in which Americans found themselves. He was a very interesting speaker.)

There are many different individuals and groups around who claim that the federal income tax is either unconstitutional or illegal for a variety of reasons. Many of them encourage others to employ their methods to stop paying it. Moreover, there are many other individuals who simply just stop paying federal income taxes.

Schiff did not believe that the federal income tax was unconstitutional. Rather, he believed that it was voluntary because, if it were mandatory, it would be unconstitutional. And because it was voluntary, the way that the government was imposing it and collecting it was illegal. (Schiff provided a tremendous amount of apparent evidence which backed up his allegations.) So no one should even be required to file an income tax return. However, Schiff knew that many people had been convicted for failing to file tax returns, so he devised a method for filing one while declaring that the individual was not liable for the tax. He called it the "Zero Income Tax Return."

On a Zero Income Tax Return, the filer declared that he or she did not have any "income" under the legal definition of that word (according to Schiff) and that he or she was not "liable" to pay federal income taxes. Therefore, the individual did not owe any. Then the filer would append two to three pages to the return listing all of the various constitutional and legal reasons that he or she did not owe income taxes. Many subscribers to Schiff's beliefs successfully filed Zero Income Returns with the I.R.S., some of them for up to 6 years with no major negative repercussions from them or the Justice Department! And some even received refunds from the I.R.S. after doing so!

So I found myself in a situation in which I saw thousands of Schiff's followers filing Zero Income Tax Returns with the I.R.S. and none of them suffering any negative repercussions from the I.R.S. And some of them even received refunds from them! In addition, Schiff explained everything so comprehensively that virtually all of it made sense to me. All of this taken as a whole finally convinced me in 1996 that I could also legally stop paying federal income taxes as well. So I did. I also filed amended tax returns for the previous two years and asked for refunds of those taxes as well. I was finally taking a patriotic, proactive stand in an attempt to expose some of the corruption being perpetrated by the federal government!

At the time that I decided to stop paying federal income taxes, I was working as a real estate broker in my own small agency in Auburn, New Hampshire. I had been working diligently for a few years to try to build it up. However, over the years prior to that, I had gotten behind on the federal income taxes that I owed, as had so many other Americans across the country. So I was making monthly payments to the I.R.S. When I realized, (according to Schiff) that I did not owe any of those taxes in the first place, I told the I.R.S. that I was no longer going to make those monthly payments to them anymore!

The I.R.S. Put Me Out of Business!

It only took a few months after I informed the I.R.S. of that for them to seize my bank accounts (business and personal) and instruct each of my real estate clients that if I were to broker the sale of their properties for them, they were not to pay me! Instead, they were to forward my commission money to the I.R.S. to go toward the payment of my back taxes. In effect, the I.R.S. put my real estate agency out of business!

In hindsight, I probably should have capitulated to the I.R.S. and continued making monthly payments to them in order to save the business that I had worked so hard to build up. However, Schiff was such a persuasive and dynamic speaker that he thoroughly convinced me that I was in the right and that it was the government which was acting illegally. He also convinced me that I could sue the I.R.S. for putting my real estate agency out of business and win! So I decided not to capitulate to them. Instead, I stood up to them!

I Began Disseminating Schiff's Information to Others

I then began doing everything that I could think of to try to disseminate Schiff's information to others. I conducted my own 3-hour income tax seminars seminars at a local hotel; I was interviewed on television, radio, newspapers, and magazines; I set up my own website at zeroincometax.com disseminating Schiff's information and selling videotapes of my seminars; I erected a large sign in front of my home/office on a very busy road advertising that anyone could legally stop paying income taxes; I had many letters-to-the-editor and opinion pieces published; I advertised my seminars; I assisted individuals in filing Schiff-style tax returns with the latest attachments explaining to the I.R.S. why they believed that they did not owe income taxes; I assisted individuals in responding to notices that some of them received from the I.R.S. after they filed a Zero Income Tax Return, etc. I also assisted Schiff in conducting his seminars whenever he conducted one in the New England area.

I also filed civil lawsuits against the I.R.S. agents who seized my bank accounts and put my real estate agency out of business. Schiff had always encouraged his followers to learn the income tax laws for themselves and also to learn how the legal system worked in case they ever needed to sue the I.R.S. or defend themselves against a government lawsuit. So I learned how to apply Civil Law (as opposed to Criminal Law).

I learn some Civil law from Schiff, but most of what I learned came from an organization called the "Erwin Rommel School of Law." (Its website is Rommellaw.com.) It was named after World War II Nazi General Erwin Rommel because it was believed during that war that he was the one general who could make the most effective use of the least amount of resources. Unfortunately, the courts dismissed all of my lawsuits against the I.R.S. and against individual I.R.S. agents! However undeterred, I persevered in promoting Schiff's information.

One of the strategies that Schiff and his many followers used in the event that the I.R.S. rejected their Zero Income Tax Return and demanded money was to meet with an I.R.S. agent in his or her office and demand that he or she cite the law that made an individual liable to pay federal income taxes, to cite the legal definition of the word "income" with respect to income taxes, etc. None of the I.R.S. agents could do it. We also tape-recorded these meetings so that we had a record of them not being able to do it. I attended a number of these meetings on my own behalf and also as a witness for a few of my clients.

In years past, if the I.R.S. determined that a person owed federal income taxes, it would simply levy that person's bank account or whatever other assets that person owned in order to try to collect those taxes. However, subsequent to U.S. congressional hearings in 1996 into many serious I.R.S. infractions, Congress enacted a law which stated that before the I.R.S. could levy a person's property, the person first must be afforded a Collection Due Process (CDP) Hearing to be able to challenge the I.R.S.' levy. So I assisted a number of my clients with their filing of paperwork regarding Collection Due Process Hearings.

If the person was not satisfied with the result of that Collection Due Process Hearing, that person could then appeal the I.R.S.' decision to a U.S. District Court. Since the I.R.S. never ruled in favor of the taxpayer in a Collection Due Process Hearing, I also assisted a number of my clients with the filing of paperwork regarding their appeals of their CDP Hearing decisions.

I conducted these activities for almost five years (from 1997 to 2002), even though I was earning very little money doing so. I did so because I was thoroughly convinced that Schiff was correct in his assertions. And all the while the Justice Department never gave me any trouble, even though many times I encouraged callers to my radio interviews who thought I was doing something illegal to call the U.S. Attorney's office and report me if they believed I was doing something illegal.

Chapter 3. My Responses to 9/11

On September 11, 2001, "terrorists" hijacked commercial jetliners and crashed them into the World Trade Center in New York City and the Pentagon in Arlington County, Virginia! They also crashed another jetliner in Pennsylvania, killing all of the people aboard! I sat mesmerized while watching those events unfold that day. All tolled, almost 3000 innocent people were killed! As I stated earlier, at that time I had already spent many years watching and studying details about the inordinate amount of power and influence certain Jews were able to wield throughout the world.

During the attacks, my first thought was that officials within our own government and Israeli Zionists were somehow involved in them. At that time, the U.S. economy was in recession and I thought that a False Flag terrorist attack blamed on some other country or group might be used by U.S. government officials to try to help get us out of it by declaring war on them. In addition, I had been following the fact that Israelis had been widely castigated in the mainstream media during the previous few months. First, they had been castigated after controversial figure, General Ariel Sharon, and 1100 Israeli military and police officers interrupted Muslims while they prayed at the Temple Mount in Jerusalem (the third holiest site in Islam) and declared that the area would in the future be under perpetual Israeli control. That act caused widespread outrage and rioting among many Muslims.

Then, just before September 11th, Israelis were castigated even further in the news media when the United States' and the Israeli delegations to the United Nations' Conference on Human Rights held in Durban, South Africa walked out of that conference in protest over the efforts of many of the member countries to equate Zionism with racism. (Up until 1992, the United Nations had officially equated Zionism with racism. That year, the efforts of U.S. President George H. W. Bush [a long-time Bilderberg Group member] were instrumental in getting that long-standing designation rescinded.) So I surmised that Israeli Zionists might have orchestrated the attacks as a means of deflecting attention away from themselves.

It was only a couple of hours after those terrorist attacks that the mainstream media (MSM) were in a lock-stepped frenzy accusing Osama bin Laden for the attacks. They were doing so even though bin Laden denied his involvement in them. (It would have been unusual for bin Laden to deny his involvement if he were actually involved because Muslim terrorists are usually quick to claim responsibility for their actions.) But I knew that bin Laden was a long-time C.I.A. asset—a relationship which began in the 1980s when he and his Mujaheddin forces were backed by the United States in their struggle to oust Russia from Afghanistan.

I also knew that bin Laden was the latest whipping boy for U.S. presidents Clinton and George W. Bush and the mainstream media to accuse of committing dastardly deeds in order to deflect attention away from what was really going on in the world. Before bin Laden, it was Saddam Hussein; before him, it was Muammar Gaddafi, before him, it was Abu Nidal; before them, it was the Soviet Union. (Since bin Laden, the West's contrived Common Enemies have been the Taliban, al Qaida, and now the Islamic State. Isn't it interesting how these well-equipped, well-financed, well-trained terrorist groups have seemed to pop up out of nowhere?)

I believe that wealthy oligarchs (many of whom are war profiteers) learned a long time ago that they could keep their "War Machine" rolling and earn colossal profits for themselves by always having a boogie-man enemy of the United States and Western civilization. I believe that subsequent to the Industrial Revolution of the late 1800s and early 1900s, the newly-wealthy industrialists of that time were instrumental in orchestrating the Russian Revolution and the later creation of the Soviet Union as the west's "Common Enemy." (What else would explain the ability of wealthy industrialist Armand Hammer, CEO of Occidental Petroleum, to fly his plane into the city of

Moscow in the Soviet Union whenever he wanted to? He was able to accomplish that feat even during the purported "Cold War" between the United State and the Soviet Union!)

I also believe that the reason that the United States was dragged into World War II via the pretextual bombing of Pearl Harbor, Hawaii was to save the Soviet Union from the ever-expanding Nazi regime. Adolf Hitler and the Nazis would have eventually annihilated the Soviet Union and the wealthy oligarchs could not have that! The wealthy oligarchs also learned a long time ago that they could control people by controlling the information that they receive. So they bought all of the major news and entertainment media. They also bought off many of our elected "leaders!"

As I stated earlier, my first thoughts were that Israeli Zionists were behind the attacks as a way to deflect attention away from all of the negative press they had been receiving in the global mainstream media. So I began writing and distributing e-mail to that effect.

The first place that I stated something was in a Yahoo! discussion group to which I belonged. It was a group for followers of Irwin Schiff and was called the Zero Income Filers ("ZIF") group. Discussion within that group was limited to the subject of filing federal income tax returns with the Internal Revenue Service as Mr. Schiff recommended that they be filed. For members who wished to discuss topics other than income taxes, a sister group, Zero Income Talk ("Talk") had been formed.

At 10:22 a.m. on September 11, 2001, another member of the group wrote the following:

> "As I watch the surreal events unfolding in New York and Washington, I can't help but wonder what path America will be taken down. Unfortunately, it is cataclysmic events such as these that force historic and abrupt changes in our culture and lives."

At 12:24 p.m., I responded to that post with:

"It is even sadder to think that this may have been orchestrated by the Government in order to prop up a collapsing economy and because of Israel's inability to stop the violence in that country.

I almost wrote a 'letter to the editor' the other day about the propensity for Presidents named Bush to initiate a war (such as the Persian Gulf War) when the economy gets bad and to expect another one in the near future. I wish I had written it.

Steven A. Swan

P.S. Sorry about the off-topic post. I should have sent it to zeroincometalk."

At 1:45 p.m., the moderator of the group posted a message stating-

"[ZIF] posting rules suspended for the rest of the day to allow discussion of the attack on our country."

I responded at 4:56 p.m. to that posting with-

"In addition to the reasons I cited earlier for the attack by the U.S. Government on its own people in order to blame Arab terrorists (to bolster a collapsing economy and because Israel has been unable to stem the violence in that country), don't forget about all of the negative press that Israel has been receiving lately about Zionism being equated with racism. So much so that the United States and Israel walked out of the Summit on Racism in South Africa the other day.

Up until 1992, the U.N. did equate Zionism with racism. Up until the other President Bush's puppet-masters forced him to employ the force of the U.S. Government to get it rescinded that is.

It is amazing that a country can become so ruthless that it will murder thousands of its own citizens for political gain. And because the powers-that-be also control the media, 99.9% of Americans won't even realize what happened."

Later, I began to see the bigger picture-that the attacks were probably a False Flag operation orchestrated by the Zionists and blamed on their enemies in the Middle East (Arabs and Muslims) as a pretext to implementing a much larger U.S. military presence in the Middle East. That outcome would have been beneficial not only to the Zionists, but also to the U.S. Military-Industrial Complex, of which President Dwight D. Eisenhower had warned Americans at the conclusion of his presidency.

It was not inconceivable that Israeli and American pro-Israel Zionists could have convinced "former" C.I.A. operative Osama bin Laden to dupe 19 Arabs into carrying out terrorist attacks against the "Great Satan" (United States) when the real beneficiaries would have been the Zionists and the Military/Industrial Complex of the United States. The many Zionist Neo-Conservatives[3] in the George W. Bush Administration (C.I.A. Director George Tenet, F.B.I. Director Louis Freeh, Deputy Secretary of Defense Paul Wolfowitz, 1st Assistant Secretary of Defense for Global Strategic Affairs Richard Perle, Speechwriter David Frum, Under Secretary of Defense Richard Armitage, National Security Council operative Elliot Abrams, White House Press Secretary Ari Fleischer, Pentagon Defense Policy Board member, Kenneth Adelman head of the Defense Department's Office of Special Plans Douglas Feith, etc.) and in the media (co-founder of *The Weekly Standard* magazine William Kristol, *U.S. News and World* Report owner Mortimer Zuckerman, political commentator and columnist Charles Krauthammer, veteran *60* Minutes correspondent Mike Wallace, *Wall Street Journal* editor and columnist Max Boot, and many more) were certainly in favor of an expanded U.S. military presence in the Middle East for their Zionist interests.

---

3 Prior to the Neo-Conservatives taking over the Republican Party, it was primarily comprised of old-school conservatives like Barry Goldwater, Ronald Reagan, Pat Buchanan, etc. Then, over time, the Zionist Neo-Conservatives gradually took over the party and converted it into a primarily pro-Zionist one.

On September 20, 2001, I wrote the following letter-to-the editor to the Union Leader newspaper of Manchester, New Hampshire: (I have also reproduced this letter in plain text at the end of it so that users of any device will be able to read it.)

Steven Swan

From: "Steven Swan" <stevenswan@earthlink.net>
To: "Union Leader" <TheUL@aol.com>
Sent: Thursday, September 20, 2001 9:40 AM
Subject: Letter to the Editor

September 20, 2001

To the Editor:

You won't hear about it from the controlled, mainstream media, but there are many patriotic Americans who believe that Israel had the most to gain from the recent terrorist attacks on the United States and that the Israeli Mossad was directly responsible. By orchestrating an attack on the United States and blaming it on Islamic terrorists, Israel would be able to rally the American people to get behind them in their battle against the Arabs in the Middle East.

Remember that at the time of the attacks, Israel was being sharply criticized for the way it was handling all of the violence in that country; violence which was instigated by Ariel Sharon when he and 1100 armed troops visited the Temple Mount on one of the Moslem holy days so that he could destabilize the region in order to be elected Prime Minister. (This is the same Ariel Sharon who was personally responsible for the slaughter of 1200 elderly men, women and children in the Palestinian refugee camps of Shabra and Chantilla in Lebanon in 1982 after he assured the Palestinian men that they would be safe.) Remember also that at the time of the terrorist attacks on this country, Israel and the United States had boycotted the U.N. Conference on Racism in South Africa because many countries were calling for a U.N. declaration that Zionism is a form of racism—a designation which it held at the U.N. until 1992. At the time of the terrorist attacks on the United States, Israel was receiving a lot of negative publicity in the mainstream media.

But how could the Israeli Mossad, an organization which is vehemently despised by Arabs throughout the world, entice at least 19 of them to participate in a suicidal terrorist attack on the United States? Perhaps by employing a former CIA operative like Osama Bin Laden to deceive them into believing that they were attacking what they refer to as "The Great Satan", when in reality they were being used as unwitting tools of the Israeli Mossad.

Steven A. Swan, P.O. Box 453, Auburn, NH 03032 (603) 483-5610

To the Editor:

You won't hear about it from the controlled, mainstream media, but there are many patriotic Americans who believe that Israel had the most to gain from the recent terrorist attacks on the United States and that the Israeli Mossad was directly responsible. By orchestrating an attack on the United States and blaming it on Islamic terrorists, Israel would be able to rally the American people to get behind them in their battle against the Arabs in the Middle East.

Remember that at the time of the attacks, Israel was being sharply criticized for the way it was handling all of the violence in that country; violence which was instigated by Ariel Sharon when he and 1100 armed troops visited the

Temple Mount on one of the Moslem holy days so that he could destabilize the region in order to be elected Prime Minister. (This is the same Ariel Sharon who was personally responsible for the slaughter of 1200 elderly men, women and children in the Palestinian refugee camps of Shabra and Chantilla in Lebanon in 1982 after he assured the Palestinian men that they would be safe.) Remember also that at the time of the terrorist attacks on this country, Israel and the United States had boycotted the U.N. Conference on Racism in South Africa because many countries were calling for a U.N. declaration that Zionism is a form of racism-a designation which it held at the U.N. until 1992. At the time of the terrorist attacks on the United States, Israel was receiving a lot of negative publicity in the mainstream media.

But how could the Israeli Mossad, an organization which is vehemently despised by Arabs throughout the world, entice at least 19 of them to participate in a suicidal terrorist attack on the United States? Perhaps by employing a former CIA operative like Osama Bin Laden to deceive them into believing that they were attacking what they refer to as 'The Great Satan", when in reality they were being used as unwitting tools of the Israeli Mossad.

Steven A. Swan, P.O. Box 453, Auburn, NH 03032 (603) 483-5610"

      Also on September 20, 2001, I posted the following message with the subject line of "Who Benefits" to both the Zero Income Filers (ZIF) and Investigating Curious Evidence (ICE) Yahoo discussion groups. (Investigating Curious Evidence was another Yahoo! discussion group to which I belonged.) The post includes an article by Willis Carto from the *American Free Press* newspaper entitled "America Mourns."

I have also reproduced many of the following submissions in plain text at the end of them so that users of any device will be able to read them.

(On some of the following figures, you might see the word "Exhibit" or you might see numbered tabs on an edge of a page. That is because these figures were exhibits in a motion I filed with the court in a subsequent court proceeding in which I was a party.)

Steven Swan

From: "Steven Swan" <stevenswan@earthlink.net>
Sent: Thursday, September 20, 2001 12:01 PM
Subject: Who Benefits?

There are many people who believe that Israel stood to benefit the most from the United States' involvement in a war against Islam and that the terrorist attacks last week were perpetrated by the Israeli Mossad in order to draw America into a war. Here is an editorial by the publisher of the American Free Press, which has taken the place of The Spotlight now that the Government has silenced it. It might take a few seconds for the article to load.

Steven A. Swan
http://www.zeroincometax.com
Petition Drive Exposing the Fraud of the Federal Income Tax

AmericanFreePres

★ ★ ★ ★ ★ ★ ★ ★ ★ ★ For Life & Liberty . . . Against the New World Order ★ ★ ★ ★ ★ ★ ★

American Free Press
- About AFP
- Censored Stories
- Editorials
- The New World Order
- Illegal Immigration
- Eye on Bilderberg
- Coming Police State
- Corruption Exposed
- What's Up in Congress?
- News You Missed
- Lane's Law
- The Ryan Report
- Truth Hurts
- Letters to the Editor
- Vote Reform
- Finances
- Mideast Turmoil
- Race Relations
- Foreign Relations
- NAFTA/GATT
- What's On Your Mind

AFP Photo Gallery
Archives
Classifieds
Subscribing
Advertising in AFP
E-Mail Us
Links
Patriot Action Center

PLEASE NOTE

America Mourns

Thousands Killed; Many More Missing in Brutal Attacks

The people behind the recent terrible act of terrorism that took the lives of thousands of innocent people should be brought to justice. As with any investigation, a good place to start is by asking: who benefits from this heinous crime?

Exclusive to American Free Press

By W. A. Carto

There is no better method to find a criminal than cui bono, the ancient Roman legal principle, meaning "Who benefits?" This principle is as important to the problem of discovering the criminals behind the day of terrorism, Sept. 11, as it is in a simple murder case.

If the deed was the responsibility of any Arab or Muslim group, then the motive was pure hatred of the United States. And why do they hate us so? Any one should know the answer to that question; it is because of the totally one-sided policy of this nation in regard to the conflict between the artificial nation of Israel-an American creation-and its neighbors.

But if there is a more pragmatic motive for the horrible crime, for example, to induce even stronger support of Israel, even more money for that pampered nation, even more military supportthen the whole picture abruptly changes.

The pet culprit of the mass media is a little character hiding out in a cave somewhere in Afghanistan-Osama bin Laden. This man-according to the media-is so powerful, wealthy, well-connected and smart that he was able to bring together hundreds of skilled technicians and faultlessly execute one of the most devastating military strikes of all time, and to do it without being detected in advance by any of this nation's intelligence agencies or the Mossad-the Israeli intelligence and action arm that is known to have its spies infiltrated into every anti-Israel group in the world.

Veteran FBI agent Ted Gunderson told American Free Press:

EXHIBIT 4

10/6/03

The AFP Site is still under construction. Many of the sections above are not yet active.

There is no way that our U.S. intelligence did not know about this strike in advance. To skyjack four or five planes at the same time and have each gang of skyjackers operating precisely on schedule and with coordinated instructions would take 70 to 100 people involved at the least. Our intelligence and the Mossad would have to know about this in advance.

OKLAHOMA CITY PARALLEL

Judging from the bombing of the Oklahoma City federal building, every honest student knows very well that not only the FBI but the CIA, BATF, the Mossad and sundry undercover groups knew about it in advance. This subject was copiously covered and discussed by the former Spotlight newspaper as well as by experts, including Gen. Ben Partin, Hoppy Heidelberg and bombing survivor V. Z. Lawton at the Second **Barnes Review International Conference on Authentic History and the First Amendment** last June. (Video and audio tapes of their presentations are available from **The Barnes Review**. Call 1-877-773-9077 for details.)

The Sept. 11 terror was a much bigger event than the Oklahoma City bombing and far more people had to be involved. Did the CIA-Mossad know about it in advance? If they did, why did they not prevent the horrible crime? Is it because they very well knew what the political results would be an escalation of America's all-out support of Israel?

DISASTER

Everyone-even pro-Zionists-are aware that Ariel Sharon, Israel's prime minister, is capable of the most atrocious and heinous terrorism. This war criminal is generally recognized as a ruthless leader whose history shows that he stops at nothing to attain his ends. Would he be capable of such murderous treachery against the "best ally" of Israel if it would gain him even greater support from that blindly loyal ally?

As responsible observers have been repeating for almost a century, America's internationalist policy has brought nothing but disaster to this once-great and once-proud nation, and it will continue to bring the same. The people of America are under the sway of evil forces which use our strength and credulity to waste us, trash our heritage and murder our future. Our enemies are powerful and control the rest of the media, Congress and the president. As our country reels from disaster to disaster like a confirmed drunk, we seek repair by drinking more of the same poison that has caused our distress.

May God help America. H

"Subject: Who Benefits?

There are many people who believe that Israel stood to benefit the most from the United States' involvement in a war against Islam and that the terrorist attacks last week were perpetrated by the Israeli Mossad in order to draw America into a war. Here is an editorial by the publisher of the American Free Press, which has taken the place of The Spotlight now that the Government has silenced it. It might take a few seconds for the article to load.

Steven A. Swan

America Mourns

Thousands Killed; Many More Missing in Brutal Attacks

The people behind the recent terrible act of terrorism that took the lives of thousands of innocent people should be brought to justice. As with any investigation, a good place to start is by asking: who benefits from this heinous crime?

Exclusive to American Free Press

By W. A. Carto

There is no better method to find a criminal than cui bono, the ancient Roman legal principle, meaning "Who benefits?" This principle is as important to the problem of discovering the criminals behind the day of terrorism, Sept. 11, as it is in a simple murder case.

If the deed was the responsibility of any Arab or Muslim group, then the motive was pure hatred of the United States. And why do they hate us so? Any one should know the answer to that question; it is because of the totally one-sided policy of this nation in regard to the conflict between the artificial nation of Israel-an American creation-and its neighbors.

But if there is a more pragmatic motive for the horrible crime, for example, to induce even stronger support of Israel, even more money for that pampered nation, even more military support, then the whole picture abruptly changes.

The pet culprit of the mass media is a little character hiding out in a cave somewhere in Afghanistan-Osama bin Laden. This man-according to media-is so powerful, wealthy, well-connected and smart that he was able to bring together hundreds of skilled technicians and faultlessly execute one of the most devastating military strikes of all time, and to do it without being detected in advance by any of this nation's intelligence agencies or the Mossad-the Israeli action and intelligence arm that is known to have its spies infiltrated into every anti-Israel group in the world.

Veteran FBI agent Ted Gunderson told American Free Press:

There is no way that our U.S. intelligence did not know about this strike in advance. To skyjack four or five planes at the same time and have each gang of skyjackers operating precisely on schedule and with coordinated instructions would take up to 70 to 100 people involved at the least. Our intelligence and the Mossad would have to know about this in advance.

OKLAHOMA CITY PARALLEL

Judging from the bombing of the Oklahoma City federal building, every honest student knows very well that not only the FBI but the CIA, BATF, the Mossad and sundry undercover groups knew about it in advance. This subject was copiously covered and discussed by the former Spotlight newspaper as well as by experts, including Gen. Ben Partin, Hoppy Heidleberg and bombing survivor V.Z. Lawton at the Second Barnes Review International Conference on Authentic History and the First Amendment last June. (Video and audio tapes of their presentations are available from the Barnes Review. Call 1-877-773-9077 for details.)

The Sept. 11 terror was a much bigger event than the Oklahoma City bombing and far more people had to be involved. Did the CIA-Mossad know about it in advance? If they did, why did they not prevent the horrible crime? Is it because they very well knew what the political results would be-an escalation of America's all-out support of Israel?

DISASTER

Everyone-even pro-Zionists-are aware that Ariel Sharon, Israel's prime minister, is capable of the most atrocious and heinous terrorism. This war criminal is generally recognized as a ruthless leader whose history shows that he stops at nothing to attain his ends. Would he be capable of such murderous treachery against the "best ally" of Israel if it would gain him even greater support from that blindly loyal ally?

As responsible observers have been repeating for almost a century, America's internationalist policy has brought nothing but disaster to this once-great and once-proud nation, and it will continue to bring the same. The people of the Americas are under the sway of evil forces which use our strength and credulity to waste us, trash our heritage and murder our future. Our enemies are powerful and control the rest of the media, Congress and the president. As our country reels from disaster to disaster like a confirmed drunk, we seek repair by drinking more of the same poison that has caused our distress.

May God help America. H

Also on September 20, 2001, I posted the following to the ICE Yahoo! Group: It included an article entitled "Was Israel involved in the WTC and Pentagon terror attacks?", which was posted on the Cyberia.com website (www.thisiscyberia.com).

Steven Swan

From: "Steven Swan" <stevenswan@earthlink.net>
To: "ICE" <ice@iresist.com>
Sent: Thursday, September 20, 2001 12:16 PM
Subject: More Information on the Israeli Mossad

ICE,

I would discount this article as far as Jews being forewarned of the terrorist attacks, but I think that the information about the Israeli Mossad's possible involvement needs more scrutiny. This article might take a few seconds to load.

Steven A. Swan
http://www.zeroincometax.com
Petition Drive Exposing the Fraud of the Federal Income Tax

this is cyberia.com

This article was printed from Cyberia, located at www.thisiscyberia.com

Was Israel involved in the WTC and Pentagon terror attacks?
Wednesday, September 19, 2001

Mossad planned strike?

Several days after the terrorist attacks on New York and Washington DC, reports emerged that some 4,000 Israelis working at the World Trade Center did not show up for work on the day of the aircraft blasts.

A Muslim sheikh living in England commenting during a BBC news broadcast added that 40 Jewish Pentagon staff members did not show up for work on 11 September. The sheikh said it would not surprise him if it was discovered that the Mossad (the Israeli secret service) was behind the attacks.

Last Saturday's news broadcast on several local television networks - including the National Broadcasting Network (NBN), state-owned Tele-Liban, Hizbullah's Manar TV and Qatar's al Jazeera satellite station - reported the same figures during their evening newscasts.

No official source of information was mentioned in any of the news briefs, although the networks reported the Israeli secret service warned Israelis to stay away from several sites in the US.

Meanwhile, Israeli newspaper the Jerusalem Post reported that Mossad officials traveled to Washington last month to warn the CIA and FBI that there would be a major operation taking place in the US' major cities.

The Israeli secret service allegedly offered no specific information about the targets but linked the attacks to Osama bin Laden and told the Americans there were strong grounds for suspecting Iraqi involvement, the paper reported.

According to media reports, many Israelis worked in the high tech companies and trade agencies in the twin towers. Israeli daily Yediot Ahronot reported that some Israeli companies had offices in the WTC, but Israeli Channel Two television discredited this claim.

Thus far, no Israelis have been located among the injured or deceased in any of the New York City hospitals.

Israelis warned of attacks?

EXHIBIT 5

10/6/03

Meanwhile, Arab diplomatic sources revealed to the Jordanian Al Watan newspaper that Israelis remained absent from work that fateful day based on information from the Shabak, the Israeli general security apparatus.

According to the newspaper, American officials are requesting an explanation of how the Israeli government learned of the attacks before they occurred and why it refrained from informing the US authorities of the information.

Manar TV reported that suspicions increased further after Yediot Ahronot reported the Shabak prevented Premier Ariel Sharon from traveling to New York to participate in a festival organized by Zionist organizations in support of "Israel."

Israelis arrested for 'puzzling behavior'

Meanwhile, five Israelis who had worked for a moving company based in New Jersey, are being held in US prisons for what the FBI described as "puzzling behavior" following last Tuesday's attacks.

The five are expected to be deported soon, reported the Israeli Ha'aretz newspaper.

The families of the five, the paper reported, said their sons had been questioned by the FBI for hours on end, kept in solitary confinement for three days, humiliated, stripped of their clothes and blindfolded.

"When they finally let my son make a phone call to a friend, he told him he had been tortured by the FBI in a basement," the mother of one of the young men told Ha'aretz. "He was stripped to his underwear, blindfolded and questioned for 14 hours [on suspicion of] working for the Mossad."

Seven FBI agents later stormed the apartment of one of the Israelis, searched it and questioned his roommate. The Israeli owner of the moving company, who is a US citizen, was also questioned.

It is not yet clear the extent to which the five detained Israelis are implicated in the attacks and the US maintains that bin Laden is their prime suspect.

The US Attorney-General, John Ashcroft, said investigators are following up on 4,700 leads.

Taliban demand evidence of bin Laden's guilt - plus other stories

"Subject: More information on the Israeli Mossad

ICE,

I would discount this article as far as Jews being forewarned of the terrorist attacks, but I think that the information about the Israeli Mossad's possible involvement needs more scrutiny. This article might take a few seconds to load.

Steven A. Swan
http://www.zeroincometax.com
Petition Drive Exposing the Fraud of the Federal Income Tax

This is cyberia.com

This article was printed from Cyberia, located at www.thisiscyberia.com

Was Israel involved in the WTC and Pentagon terror attacks?

Wednesday, September 19, 2001

Several days after the terrorist attacks on New York and Washington DC, reports emerged that some 4,000 Israelis working at the World Trade Center did not show up for work on the day of the aircraft blasts.

A Muslim sheikh living in England commenting during a BBC news broadcast added that 40 Jewish Pentagon staff members did not show up for work on 11 September. The sheikh said it would not surprise him if it was discovered that the Mossad (the Israeli secret service) was behind the attacks.

Last Saturday's news broadcast on several local television networks – including the National Broadcasting Network (NBN), state-owned Tere-Liban, Hizbullah's Manar TV and Qatar'st al Jazeera satellite station - reported the same figures during their evening newscasts.

No official source of information was mentioned in any of the news briefs, although the networks reported the Israeli secret service warned Israelis to stay away from several sites in the US.

Meanwhile, Israeli newspaper the Jerusalem Post reported that Mossad officials traveled to Washington last month to warn the CIA and FBI that there would be a major operation taking place in the US' major cities.

The Israeli secret service allegedly offered no specific information about the targets but linked the attacks to Osama bin Laden and told the Americans there were strong grounds for suspecting Iraqi involvement, the paper reported.

According to media reports, many Israelis worked in the high tech companies and trade agencies in the twin towers. Israeli daily Yediot Ahronot reported that some Israeli companies had offices in the WTC, but Israeli Channel Two television discredited this claim.

Thus far, no Israelis have been located among the injured or deceased in any of the New York City hospitals.

Israelis warned of attacks?

Meanwhile, Arab diplomatic sources revealed to the Jordanian Al Watan newspaper that Israelis remained absent from work that fateful day based on information from the Shabak, the Israeli general security apparatus.

According to the newspaper, American officials are requesting an explanation of how the Israeli government learned of the attacks before they occurred and why it refrained from informing the US authorities of the information.

Manar TV reported that suspicions increased further after Yediot Ahronot reported the Shabak prevented Premier Ariel Sharon from traveling to New York to participate in a festival organized by Zionist organizations in support of "Israel."

Israelis arrested for 'puzzling behavior'

Meanwhile, five Israelis who had worked for a moving company based in New Jersey, are being held in US prisons for what the FBI described as "puzzling behavior" following last Tuesday's attacks.

The five are expected to be deported soon, reported the Israeli Ha'aretz newspaper.

The families of the five, the paper reported, said their sons had been questioned by the FBI for hours on end, kept in solitary confinement for three days, humiliated, stripped of their clothes and blindfolded.

"When they finally let my son make a phone call to a friend, he told him he had been tortured by the FBI in a basement," the mother of one of the young men told Ha'aretz. "He was stripped to his underwear, blindfolded and questioned for 14 hours [on suspicion of] working for the Mossad."

Seven FBI agents later stormed the apartment of one of the Israelis, searched it and questioned his roommate. The Israeli owner of the moving company, who is a US citizen was also questioned.

It is not yet clear the extent to which the five detained Israelis are implicated in the attacks and the US maintains that bin Laden is their prime suspect.

The US Attorney-General, John Ashcroft, said investigators are following up on 4,700 leads.

<u>Taliban demand evidence of bin Laden's guilt-plus other stories</u>"

On September 24, 2001, I made the following post to the Zero Income Filers Yahoo Group:

From: "Steven Swan <stevenswan@earthlink.net>

To: <zeroincomefilers@yahoogroups.com>

Sent: Monday, September 24, 2001 6:50 AM

Subject Re:[ZIF]Slander-by-Association

Let me see if I have this right. The Mossad is good and the ADL is bad. This doesn't seem to make much sense since the ADL does a tremendous amount of information gathering for the Mossad and the two are joined at the hip.

Steven A. Swan

--- Original Message ---

From:@

To: <zeroincomefilers@yahoogroups.com>

Sent Saturday, September 22, 2001 2:28 PM

Subject Re: [ZIFI Slander-by-Association

> The ADL is one of the most dangerous groups in America. They are

> statists pure and simple.

>Don

Also on September 24, 2001, I emailed the following letter-to-the-editor to the Weirs Times newspaper in Weirs Beach, New Hampshire:

Steven Swan

From: "Steven Swan" <stevenswan@earthlink.net>
To: "Weirs Times" <weirst@worldpath.net>
Sent: Monday, September 24, 2001 11:08 AM
Subject: Letter to the Editor
September 24, 2001

To the Editor:

You won't hear about it from the controlled, mainstream media, but there are many patriotic Americans who believe that Israel had the most to gain from the recent terrorist attacks on the United States and that the Israeli Mossad was directly responsible. By orchestrating an attack on the United States and blaming it on Islamic terrorists, Israel would be able to rally the American people to get behind them in their battle against the Arabs in the Middle East.

Remember that at the time of the attacks, Israel was being sharply criticized for the way it was handling all of the violence in that country; violence which was instigated by Ariel Sharon when he and 1100 armed troops visited the Temple Mount on one of the Moslem holy days so that he could destabilize the region in order to be elected Prime Minister. (This is the same Ariel Sharon who was personally responsible for the slaughter of 1200 elderly men, women and children in the Palestinian refugee camps of Shabra and Chantilla in Lebanon in 1982 after he assured the Palestinian men that they would be safe.) Remember also that at the time of the terrorist attacks on this country, Israel and the United States had boycotted the U.N. Conference on Racism in South Africa because many countries were calling for a U.N. declaration that Zionism is a form of racism—a designation which it held at the U.N. until 1992. At the time of the terrorist attacks on the United States, Israel was receiving a lot of negative publicity in the mainstream media.

But how could the Israeli Mossad, an organization which is vehemently despised by Arabs throughout the world, entice at least 19 of them to participate in a suicidal terrorist attack on the United States? Perhaps by employing a former CIA operative like Osama Bin Laden to deceive them into believing that they were attacking what they refer to as "The Great Satan", when in reality they were being used as unwitting tools of the Israeli Mossad.

Steven A. Swan, P.O. Box 453, Auburn, NH 03032 (603) 483-5610

"To the Editor:

You won't hear about it from the controlled, mainstream media, but there are many patriotic Americans who believe that Israel had the most to gain from the recent terrorist attacks on the United States and that the Israeli Mossad was directly responsible. By orchestrating an attack on the United States and blaming it on Islamic terrorists, Israel would be able to rally the American people to get behind them in their battle against the Arabs in the Middle East.

Remember that at the time of the attacks, Israel was being sharply criticized for the way it was handling all of the violence in that country; violence which was instigated by Ariel Sharon when he and 1100 armed troops visited the Temple Mount on one of the Moslem holy days so that he could destabilize the region in order to be elected Prime

Minister. (This is the same Ariel Sharon who was personally responsible for the slaughter of 1200 elderly men, women and children in the Palestinian refugee camps of Shabra and Chantilla in Lebanon in 1982 after he assured the Palestinian men that they would be safe.) Remember also that at the time of the terrorist attacks on this country, Israel and the United States had boycotted the U.N. Conference on Racism in South Africa because many countries were calling for a U.N. declaration that Zionism is a form of racism-a designation which it held at the U.N. until 1992. At the time of the terrorist attacks on the United States, Israel was receiving a lot of negative publicity in the mainstream media.

But how could the Israeli Mossad, an organization which is vehemently despised by Arabs throughout the world, entice at least 19 of them to participate in a suicidal terrorist attack on the United States? Perhaps by employing a former CIA operative like Osama Bin Laden to deceive them into believing that they were attacking what they refer to as 'The Great Satan", when in reality they were being used as unwitting tools of the Israeli Mossad.

Steven A. Swan, P.O. Box 453, Auburn, NH 03032 (603) 483-5610"

On September 27, 2001, I emailed the following letter to one of my U.S. senators, Robert C. Smith (R-NH).

Steven Swan

From: "Steven Swan" <stevenswan@earthlink.net>
To: "Senator Robert C. Smith (R-NH)" <opinion@smith.senate.gov>
Sent: Thursday, September 27, 2001 4:35 PM
Subject: Terrorist Charade

Dear Senator Smith:

Please don't get caught up in the frenzy against Muslims whipped up by the Zionist controlled, mainstream media and their lackeys in Government. There are many patriotic Americans who realize that Israel had the most to gain from the United States being drawn into a protracted war with Islam and who can see through the charade. The United States should be going after the Israeli Mossad for committing these heinous crimes rather than Islamic fundamentalists.

Remember that at the time of the attacks, Israel was being sharply criticized for the way it was handling all of the violence in that country; violence which was instigated by Ariel Sharon when he and 1100 armed troops visited the Temple Mount on one of the Moslem holy days so that he could destabilize the region in order to be elected Prime Minister. (This is the same Ariel Sharon who was personally responsible for the slaughter of 1200 elderly men, women and children in the Palestinian refugee camps of Shabra and Chantilla in Lebanon in 1982 after he assured the Palestinian men that they would be safe.) Remember also that at the time of the terrorist attacks on this country, Israel and the United States had boycotted the U.N. Conference on Racism in South Africa because many countries were calling for a U.N. declaration that Zionism is a form of racism—a designation which it held at the U.N. until 1992. At the time of the terrorist attacks on the United States, Israel was receiving a lot of negative publicity in the mainstream media.

But how could the Israeli Mossad, an organization which is vehemently despised by Arabs throughout the world, entice at least 19 of them to participate in a suicidal terrorist attack on the United States? By employing a former CIA operative like Osama Bin Laden to deceive them into believing that they were attacking what they refer to as "The Great Satan", when in reality they were being used as unwitting tools of the Israeli Mossad.

So please don't get caught up in this contrived frenzy. Go after the real perpetrators of these crimes. Thank you.

Steven A. Swan, P.O. Box 453, Auburn, NH 03032

"Subject: Terrorist Charade

Dear Senator Smith:

Please don't get caught up in the frenzy against Muslims whipped up by the Zionist controlled mainstream media and their lackeys in Government. There are many patriotic Americans who realize that Israel had the most to gain from the United States being drawn into a protracted war with Islam and who can see through the charade. The United States should be going after the Israeli Mossad for committing these heinous crimes rather than Islamic fundamentalists.

Remember that at the time of the attacks, Israel was being sharply criticized for the way it was handling all of the violence in that country; violence which was instigated by Ariel Sharon when he and 1100 armed troops visited the Temple Mount on one of the Moslem holy days so that he could destabilize the region in order to be elected Prime Minister. (This is the same Ariel Sharon who was personaly responsible for the slaughter of 1200 elderly men, women and children in the Palestinian refugee camps of Shabra and Chantilla in Lebanon in 1982 after he assured the Palestinian men that they would be safe.) Remember also that at the time of the terrorist attacks on this country, Israel and the United States had boycotted the U.N. Conference on Racism in South Africa because many countries were calling for a U.N. declaration that Zionism is a form of racism-a designation which it held at the U.N. until 1992. At the time of the terrorist attacks on the United States, Israel was receiving a lot of negative publicity in the mainstream media.

But how could the Israeli Mossad, an organization which is vehemently despised by Arabs throughout the world, entice at least 19 of them to participate in a suicidal terrorist attack on the United States? By employing a former CIA operative like Osama Bin Laden to deceive them into believing that they were attacking what they refer to as "The Great Satan", when in reality they were being used as unwitting tools of the Israeli Mossad.

So please don't get caught up in this contrived frenzy. Go after the real perpetrators of these crimes. Thank you.

Steven A. Swan, P. O. Box 453, Auburn, NH 03032"

On October 8, 2001, I began increasing the amount of correspondence I was sending to local news organizations in my area. I emailed the following letter-to-the-editor to the Boston Herald, Claremont Eagle Times, Concord Monitor, Lawrence Eagle Tribune, Nashua Telegraph, Portsmouth Herald, Union Leader, Weirs Times, and Keene Sentinel.

Steven Swan

From: "Steven Swan" <stevenswan@earthlink.net>
To: "Boston Herald" <newstips@bostonherald.com>; "Claremont Eagle Times" <etimes@cyberportal.net>; "Concord Monitor" <pbakke@cmonitor.com>; "Lawrence Eagle Tribune" <crock@eagletribune.com>; "Nashua Telegraph" <webeditor@telegraph-nh.com>; "Portsmouth Herald" <pherald@aol.com>; "Union Leader" <TheUL@aol.com>; "Weirs Times" <weirst@worldpath.net>; "Keene Sentinel" <news@keenesentinel.com>
Sent: Monday, October 08, 2001 1:23 PM
Subject: Letter to the Editor

To the Editor:

One would think that after the terrorist attacks of September 11th, the first question a freethinking person would ask is "Who stands to benefit the most from drawing the United States into a protracted war with Islam?" The answer is obvious. Israel has the most to gain. By committing a terrorist attack against the United States and then blaming it on its enemies, Israel could get the United States to fight all of its battles for it and never have to lift a finger.

However, within minutes of the attacks, the controlled media was declaring that Osama bin Laden had committed the attacks, conveniently overlooking the fact that both Saddam Hussein and Osama bin Laden were former CIA operatives who have been used many times in the past as diversions by both former Presidents Bush and Clinton whenever the need arose. Who's to say that the Israeli Mossad didn't employ bin Laden again to convince 19 Muslim extremists that they were attacking what they refer to as "The Great Satan" when in reality they were unwittingly helping Israel by dragging the United States into a war against Israel's enemies? And who other than a high-level intelligence organization like the Israeli Mossad would have known the secret codes of Air Force One that day and freaked out the president's people so badly that the president was forced to make two unscheduled stops at secure locations on his way back to Washington?

One thing you can be sure of is that these ruthless murderers will commit even more attacks (nuclear, chemical, and biological) against innocent United States citizens and blame it on Islamic extremists until we are at war with every one of Israel's enemies. And, unfortunately, the American people will believe every bit of deception the controlled, mainstream media throws at them.

Steven A. Swan
P.O. Box 453
Auburn, NH 03032
(603) 483-5610

"To the Editor:

One would think that after the terrorist attacks of September 1lth, the first question a freethinking person would ask is "Who stands to benefit the most from drawing the United States into a protracted war with Islam?" The answer is obvious. Israel has the most to gain. By committing a terrorist attack against the United States and then blaming it on its enemies, Israel could get the United States to fight all of its battles for it and never have to lift a finger.

However, within minutes of the attacks, the controlled media was declaring that Osama bin Laden had committed the attacks, conveniently overlooking the fact that both Saddam Hussein and Osama bin Laden were former CIA operatives who have been used many times in the past as diversions by both former Presidents Bush and Clinton whenever the need arose. Who's to say that the Israeli Mossad didn't employ bin Laden again to convince 19 Muslim extremists that they were attacking what they refer to as "The Great Satan" when in reality they were unwittingly helping Israel by dragging the United States into a war against Israel's enemies? And who other than a high-level intelligence organization like the Israeli Mossad would have known the secret codes of Air Force One that day and freaked out the president's people so badly that the president was forced to make two unscheduled stops at secure locations on his way back to Washington?

One thing you can be sure of is that these ruthless murderers will commit even more attacks (nuclear, chemical, and biological) against innocent United States citizens and blame it on Islamic extremists until we are at war with every one of Israel's enemies. And, unfortunately, the American people will believe every bit of deception the controlled, mainstream media throws at them.

Steven A. Swan
P. O. Box 453
Auburn, NH 03032
(603) 483-5610"

On October 26, 2001, I emailed the following article entitled 'Are Americans the Victims of a Hoax?' to Boston, Massachusetts radio talk show hosts Jay Severin and Howie Carr. I got it from the website *What Really Happened.com*.

Steven Swan

From: "Steven Swan" <stevenswan@earthlink.net>
To: "Jay Severin" <ExtremeGames@969fmtalk.com>; "Howie Carr" <howiecarr@wrko.com>
Sent: Friday, October 26, 2001 6:57 PM
Subject: Are Americans the Victims of a Hoax?

What Really Happened.com
10-23-01
http://www.whatreallyhappened.com/hoax.html

ARE AMERICANS THE VICTIMS OF A HOAX?

The time has come to stop using the flag as a blindfold, to stop waving our guns and our gods at each other, to take a close look at the facts which have emerged from the attacks on the World Trade Towers and to recognize the very real possibility, indeed probability, that We The People are the victims of a gigantic and deadly hoax.

In a normal terrorist event, the terrorists cannot wait to take credit, in order to link the violence to the sociopolitical intent of the terrorist organization. Yet the prime suspect in the New York Towers case, ex(?) CIA asset Osama Bin Laden (whose brother is one of George W. Bush's Texas business partners), has issued only two statements regarding the September 11th attacks, and both of those are denials of any involvement.

Huge problems are emerging in the official view of events. It's known that the United States was planning an invasion of Afghanistan long before the attacks on the World Trade Towers. Indeed the attacks on the World Trade Towers perfectly fit the timetable of an invasion by October stated by US officials just last summer.

The 19 names of suspected hijackers released by the FBI don't point to Afghanistan. They come from Saudi Arabia, Egypt, United Arab Emirates; all across the middle east without a focus in any one region. Indeed, even as the FBI admitting that its list of 19 names was based solely on identifications thought to have been forged, Saudi Arabia's Foreign Minister Prince Saudi Al-Faisal insisted that an investigation in Saudi Arabia showed that the 5 Saudi men were not aboard the four jetliners that crashed in New York, Virginia and Pennsylvania on September 11. "It was proved that five of the names included in the FBI list had nothing to do with what happened," Al-Faisal told the Arabic Press in Washington after meeting with U.S. President George W. Bush at the White House. A sixth identified hijacker is also reported to still be alive in Tunisia, while a 7th named man died two years ago!

In a recent development, the BBC is reporting that the transcript of a phone call made by Flight Attendant Madeline Amy Sweeney to Boston air traffic controls shows that the flight attendant gave the seat numbers occupied by the hijackers, seat numbers which were NOT the seats of the men the FBI claimed were responsible for the hijacking!

FBI Chief Robert Mueller admitted on September 20 and on September 27 that at this time the FBI has no legal proof to prove the true identities of the suicidal hijackers. Yet in the haste to move forward on the already planned war in Afghanistan, our government and the FBI (which does not have the best record for honesty in investigations to begin with, having been caught rigging lab tests, manufacturing testimony in the Vincent Foster affair, and illegally withholding/destroying evidence in the Oklahoma Bombing case) are not taking too close a look at evidence that points away from the designated suspect, ex(?) CIA asset Osama Bin Laden.

In particular, the FBI, too busy harassing political dissenters to find spies in its midst, the long rumored mole inside the White House, or plug leaks in high-tech flowing to foreign nations, has willfully and criminally ignored the implications of some vital pieces of information the FBI is itself waving around at the public.

We are being told that this crack team of terrorists, able to breeze past airport security as if it wasn't there, wound up leaving so much evidence in its wake that the bumbling Inspector Clouseau (or the FBI) could not fail to stumble over it. The locations where the terrorists supposedly stayed are so overloaded with damning materials that they resemble less a crimes scene, and more a "B" detective movie set, with vital clues always on prominent display for the cameras.

Yet another problem lies with the described actions of the hijackers themselves. We are being told on the one hand that these men were such fanatical devotees of their faith that they willingly crashed the jets they were flying into buildings. Yet on the other hand, we are being told that these same men spent the night before their planned visit to Allah drinking in strip bars, committing not just one, but two mortal sins which would keep them out of Paradise no matter what else they did. Truly devout Muslims would spend the day before a suicide attack fasting and praying. Not only does the drinking in strip bars not fit the profile of a fanatically religious

EXHIBIT 10A

10/6/03

Muslim willing to die for his cause, but the witness reports of the men in the bars are of men going out of their way to be noticed and remembered, while waving around phony identifications.

Because of the facts of the phony identifications, we don't really know who was on those planes. What we do know is that the men on those planes went to a great deal of trouble to steal the identities of Muslims, and to make sure those identities were seen and remembered, then to leave a plethora of planted clues around, such as crop dusting manuals, and letters in checked baggage (why does a terrorist about to die need to check baggage?) that "somehow" didn't get on the final, fatal, flight.

Fake terror is nothing new. According to recently released files, our government planned Operation NORTHWOODS to stage phony terror attacks against American citizens in the wake of the Bay Of Pigs, to anger Americans into support for a second invasion of Cuba. The plan was spiked by JFK. If our government has ever actually carried out such plans to stage phony terror attacks, the documents have remained classified. But given the reality of Operation NORTHWOODS, or the manner in which FDR maneuvered Japan into attacking Pearl Harbor, one cannot rule out the possibility that, once again, the people of the United States are being lied to by their own government, to manufacture consent for a war of invasion already being discussed with other nations the previous summer.

It is also quite possible, indeed likely, that the United States is being spoofed by a third party to trigger a war. It has happened before. According to Victor Ostrovsky, a defector from Israel's secret service, Mossad, Israel decided to mount a false flag operation designed to further discredit Libya, and provoke the US to attack an Arab nation. A transmitter loaded with prerecorded messages was planted in Tripoli, Libya, by a Mossad team.

The 'Trojan Horse' beamed out fake messages about Libyan-authorized bombings and planned attacks that were immediately intercepted by US electronic monitoring. Convinced by this disinformation that Libya was behind the 1986 bombing of a Berlin disco in which a US soldier died, President Ronald Reagan ordered massive air attacks on Libya, including an obvious-and illegal (under US law) attempt to assassinate Qadaffi himself. Some 100 Libyan civilians were killed, including Qadaffi's two year old daughter. Libyan officials had no idea why they were attacked.

It is worth remembering the motto of the Mossad is, "By way of deception, thou shalt do war."

Whether they were involved in the attacks or not, it cannot be doubted that Israel has benefited from the attacks in New York. While world attention is focused on what the US will do in Afghanistan, Israel has escalated its attacks against Palestinians towns. Israel has repeatedly tried to claim that Palestinians were involved in the New York attacks, hoping to bury the Palestinian cause under the rubble of the World Trade Towers.

Because of the faked IDs and stolen identities, we don't really know who planned the World Trade Towers attacks. We only know who they wanted us to blame.

And we know that the United States has been tricked in the past into bombing someone who did not deserve the attack, and that those who were bombed then embarked on what from their point of view was justified retaliation that culminated over Lockerbie. And while bombs were falling and planes were crashing, Israel was laughing at us that we had been so easily fooled into bombing Israel's targets for them.

Are we being hoaxed again, by Israel, or by our own government, or by both? It's impossible to rule that out. Right now there are a lot of people who want war. Oil companies want Afghanistan's petroleum products. Our corporations want "friendlier" markets. The CIA wants all that opium. And all those war-mongers, with all their greed and agendas, will not hesitate in the least to pour your tax dollars and your children's blood all over Afghanistan, to get those "friendlier" markets, oil, and opium.

Because of the vested interests at work here, American citizens must, more than at any other time in recent history, rely on themselves to decide what is happening in our nation. Too many of those who purport to report the "truth" to us are eager to grab more tax money and more children to pour into a war of invasion, poised at a region which has swallowed up every army that has tried to conquer it since the time of Alexander The Great.

And one more thing. Take a good look at the map of Eurasia and plot out where the United States has military deployments. They march in a straight line through the middle of Eurasia, Macedonia, Bosnia, Kosovo, Georgia, Azerbaijan, Turkmenia, Uzbekistan, Afghanistan.

The United States is prepared to cut the Russian Federation off from the oil rich middle east, and to control transportation routes from China and India into the Middle East. When Russia realizes that this is the real agenda, that's when "Dubya Dubya Three" will really

10/6/03

get going!

POSTSCRIPT: Looks like the cat is out of the bag. See http://english.pravda.ru/main/2001/10/08/17401.html

Return to top of What Really Happened

"ARE AMERICANS THE VICTIMS OF A HOAX? 10-23-01

The time has come to stop using the flag as a blindfold, to stop waving our guns and our gods at each other, to take a close look at the facts which have emerged from the attacks on the World Trade Towers and to recognize the very real possibility, indeed probability, that We The People are the victims of a gigantic and deadly hoax.

In a normal terrorist event, the terrorists cannot wait to take credit, in order to link the violence to the sociopolitical intent of the terrorist organization. Yet the prime suspect in the New York Towers case, ex (?) CIA asset Osama Bin Laden (whose brother is one of George W. Bush's Texas business partners), has issued only two statements regarding the September 11th attacks, and both of those are denials of any involvement.

Huge problems are emerging in the official view of events. It's known that the United States was planning an invasion of Afghanistan long before the attacks on the World Trade Towers. Indeed the attacks on the World Trade Towers perfectly fit the timetable of an invasion by October stated by US officials just last summer.

The 19 names of suspected hijackers released by the FBI don't point to Afghanistan. They come from Saudi Arabia, Egypt, United Arab Emirates; all across the middle east without a focus in any one region. Indeed, even as the FBI was admitting that its list of 19 names was based solely on identifications thought to have been forged, Saudi Arabia's Foreign Minister Prince Saudi Al-Faisal insisted that an investigation in Saudi Arabia showed that the 5 Saudi men were not aboard the four jetliners that crashed in New York, Virginia and Pennsylvania on September 11. "It was proved that five of the names included in the FBI list had nothing to do with what happened," Al-Faisal told the Arabic Press in Washington after meeting with U.S. President George W. Bush at the White House. A sixth identified hijacker is also reported to still be alive in Tunisia, while a 7th named man died two years ago!

In a recent development, the BBC is reporting that the transcript of a phone call made by Flight Attendant Madeline Amy Sweeney to <u>Boston air traffic controls shows that the flight attendant gave the seat numbers occupied by the hijackers, seat numbers which were NOT the seats of the men the FBI claimed were responsible for the hijacking</u>!

FBI Chief Robert Mueller admitted on September 20 and on September 27 that at this time the FBI has no legal proof to prove the true identities of the suicidal hijackers. Yet in the haste to move forward on the already planned war in Afghanistan, our government and the FBI (which does not have the best record for honesty in investigations to begin with, having been caught rigging lab tests, manufacturing testimony in the Vincent Foster affair, and illegally withholding/destroying evidence in the Oklahoma Bombing case) are not taking too close a look at evidence that points away from the designated suspect, ex(?) CIA asset Osama Bin Laden.

In particular, the FBI, too busy harassing political dissenters to find spies in its midst, the long rumored mole inside the White House, or plug leaks in high-tech flowing to foreign nations, has willfully and criminally ignored the implications of some vital pieces of information the FBI is itself waving around at the public.

We are being told that this crack team of terrorists, able to breeze past airport security as if it wasn't there, wound up leaving so much evidence in its wake that the bumbling Inspector Clouseau (or the FBI) could not fail to stumble over it. The locations where the terrorists supposedly stayed are so overloaded with damning materials that they resemble less a crimes scene, and more a "B" detective movie set, with vital clues always on prominent display for the cameras.

Yet another problem lies with the described actions of the hijackers themselves. We are being told on the one hand that these men were such fanatical devotees of their faith that they willingly crashed the jets they were flying into buildings. Yet on the other hand, we are being told that these same men spent the night before their planned visit to Allah drinking in strip bars, committing not just one, but two mortal sins which would keep them out of Paradise no matter what else they did. Truly devout Muslims would spend the day before a suicide attack fasting and praying. Not only does the drinking in strip bars not fit the profile of a fanatically religious Muslim willing to die for his cause, but the witness reports of the men in the bars are of men going out of their way to be noticed and remembered, while waving around phony identifications.

Because of the facts of the phony identifications, we don't really know who was on those planes. What we do know is that the men on those planes went to a great deal of trouble to steal the identities of Muslims, and to make sure those identities were seen and remembered, then to leave a plethora of planted clues around, such as crop dusting manuals, and letters in checked baggage (why does a terrorist about to die need to check baggage?) that "somehow' didn't get on the final, fatal, flight.

Fake terror is nothing new. According to recently released files, our government planned Operation NORTHWOODS to stage phony terror attacks against American citizens in the wake of the Bay Of Pigs, to anger Americans into support for a second invasion of Cuba. The plan was spiked by JFK. If our government has ever actually carried out such plans to stage phony terror attacks, the documents have remained classified. But given the reality of Operation NORTHWOODS, or the manner in which FDR maneuvered Japan into attacking Pearl Harbor, one cannot rule out the possibility that, once again, the people of the United States are being lied to by their own government, to manufacture consent for a war of invasion already being discussed with other nations the previous summer,

It is also quite possible, indeed likely, that the United States is being spoofed by a third party to trigger a war. It has happened before. According to Victor Ostrovsky, a defector from Israel's secret service, Mossad, Israel decided to mount a false flag operation designed to further discredit Libya, and provoke the US to attack an Arab nation. A transmitter loaded with prerecorded messages was planted in Tripoli, Libya, by a Mossad team.

The 'Trojan Horse' beamed out fake messages about Libyan-authorized bombings and planned attacks that were immediately intercepted by US electronic monitoring. Convinced by this disinformation that Libya was behind the 1986 bombing of a Berlin disco in which a US soldier died, President Ronald Reagan ordered massive air attacks on Libya, including an obvious-and illegal (under US law) attempt to assassinate Qadaffi himself. Some 100 Libyan civilians were killed, including Qadaffi's two year old daughter. Libyan officials had no idea why they were attacked.

It is worth remembering the motto of the Mossad is, "By way of deception, thou shalt do war." Whether they were involved in the attacks or not, it cannot be doubted that Israel has benefited from the attacks in New York. While world attention is focused on what the US will do in Afghanistan, Israel has escalated its attacks against Palestinians towns. Israel has repeatedly tried to claim that Palestinians were involved in the New York attacks, hoping to bury the Palestinian cause under the rubble of the World Trade Towers.

Because of the faked IDs and stolen identities, we don't really know who planned the World Trade Towers attacks. We only know who they wanted us to blame.

And we know that the United States has been tricked in the past into bombing someone who did not deserve the attack, and that those who were bombed then embarked on what from their point of view was justified retaliation that culminated over Lockerbie. And while bombs were falling and planes were crashing, Israel was laughing at us that we had been so easily fooled into bombing Israel's targets for them.

Are we being hoaxed again, by Israel, or by our own government, or by both? It's impossible to rule that out. Right now there are a lot of people who want war. Oil companies want Afghanistan's petroleum products. Our corporations want "friendlier" markets. The CIA wants all that opium. And all those war-mongers, with all their greed and agendas, will not hesitate in the least to pour your tax dollars and your children's blood all over Afghanistan, to get those "friendlier" markets, oil, and opium,

Because of the vested interests at work here, American citizens must, more than at any other time in recent history, rely on themselves to decide what is happening in our nation. Too many of-those who purport to report the 'truth' to us are eager to grab more tax money and more children to pour into a war of invasion, poised at a region which has swallowed up every army that has-tried to conquer it since the time of Alexander The Great.

And one more thing. Take a good look at the map of Eurasia and plot out where the United States has military deployments. They march in a straight line through the middle of Eurasia, Macedonia, Bosnia, Kosovo, Georgia, Azerbaijan, Turkmenia Uzbekistan, Afghanistan.

The United States is prepared to cut the Russian Federation off from the oil rich middle east, and to control transportation routes from China and India into the Middle East. When Russia realizes that this is the real agenda, that's when "Dubya Dubya Three" will really get going!

POSTSCRIPT: Looks like the cat is out of the bag. See http://english.pravda.ru/main/2001/10/08/17401.html"

Later that same day, I emailed that same story to many elected officials, news media, commentators, activists, etc. They included the following:

Steven Swan

From: "Steven Swan" <stevenswan@earthlink.net>
To: "WGIR AM" <staff@wgiram.com>; "Weirs Times" <weirst@worldpath.net>; "Wayne Green" <W2NSD@aol.com>; "Vin Suprynowicz" <Vin_Suprynowicz@lvrj.com>; "Union Leader" <writeus@theunionleader.com>; "The O'Reilly Factor" <oreilly@foxnews.com>; "Talk America Radio" <news@TalkAmerica.com>; "Shelly Uscinski" <shelly724@aol.com>; "Senator Robert C. Smith (R-NH)" <opinion@smith.senate.gov>; "Senator Judd Gregg (R-NH)" <mailbox@gregg.senate.gov>; "Sean Hannity" <hannity@foxnews.com>; "Roger Amsden" <roger@weirs.com>; "Robert T. Bevill" <rbevill@wwol.com>; "Robert Burke" <robert_p_burke_2000@yahoo.com>; "Portsmouth Herald" <pherald@aol.com>; "Peter Blute" <peterblute@wrko.com>; "Drudge Report" <drudge@drudgereport.com>; "Newsmax" <ruddyc@newsmax.com>; "New England Cable News" <feedback@necn.com>; "Nashua Telegraph" <webeditor@telegraph-nh.com>; "Media Bypass" <newsroom@4bypass.com>; "Lawrence Eagle Tribune" <crock@eagletribune.com>; "ICE" <ice@iresist.com>; "Ken Weiland" <kweiland@nhcucc.org>; "Kelley Taylore Ryan" <kryan@gwi.net>; "Keene Sentinel" <news@keenesentinel.com>; "Joe Sobran" <joe@sobran.com>; "Jim Hightower" <info@jimhightower.com>; "Jay Severin" <ExtremeGames@969fmtalk.com>; "Jack Shimek" <jshimek@ijaq.net>; "Infowars.com" <alex@infowars.com>; "Howie Carr" <howiecarr@wrko.com>; "Geoff Metcalf" <gmetcalf@worldnetdaily.com>; "Fox News" <comments@foxnews.com>; "Don Imus" <Imus@MSNBC.com>; "Don Gorman" <taylorgorman@juno.com>; "Dick Marple" <armlaw@hotmail.com>; "Dianne Gilbert" <dianneg@mail.ttlc.net>; "David Horowitz" <dhorowitz@frontpagemag.com>; "C-SPAN" <events@c-span.org>; "Congressman John E. Sununu (R-NH)" <Rep.Sununu@mail.house.gov>; "Congressman Charles Bass (R-NH)" <cbass@mail.house.gov>; "Concord Monitor" <pbakke@cmonitor.com>; "Claremont Eagle Times" <etimes@cyberportal.net>; "Chuck Harder" <charder@isgroup.net>; "Christopher Matthews" <cmatthews@sfchronicle.com>; "Charlie Rose" <charlierose@pbs.org>; "Charley Reese" <creese@orlandosentinel.com>; "Bob Cabacoff" <eexi@aol.com>; "Bob Grant" <bobgrant@wor710.com>; "Blanquita Collum" <bqview@radioamerica.org>; "Bill O'Reilly" <boreilly@worldnetdaily.com>; "Bill Gertz" <gertz@twtmail.com>; "Barry Farber" <Bfarber@ict.net>; "Art Bell" <artbell@mindspring.com>
Sent: Friday, October 26, 2001 7:05 PM
Subject: Are Americans the Victims of a Hoax?
What Really Happened.com
10-23-01
http://www.whatreallyhappened.com/hoax.html

ARE AMERICANS THE VICTIMS OF A HOAX?

"WGIR AM ; Weirs Times; Wayne Green; Vin Suprynowicz; Union Leader; The O'Reilly Factor; Talk America Radio; Shelly Uscinski; Senator Robert C. Smith (R-NH); Senator Judd Gregg (R-NH); "Sean Hannity; Roger Amsden; Robert T. Bevill; Robert Burke; "Portsrnouth Herald; "Peter Blute; "Drudge Report; "Newsmax; New England Cable News; Nashua Telegraph; Media Bypass; Lawrence Eagle Tribune; ICE; Ken Weiland; Kelley Taylore Ryan; Keene Sentinel; Joe Sobran; Jim Hightower; Jay Severin; Jack Shimek; lnfowars.com; Howie Carr; Geoff Metcalf; Fox News; Don Imus; Don Gorman; Dick Marple; Dianne Gilbert; "David Horowitz; C-SPAN; Congressman John E. Sununu (R-NH); Congressman Charles Bass (R-NH); Concord Monitor; Claremont Eagle Times; Chuck Harder; Christopher Matthews; Charlie Rose; Charley Reese; Bob Cabacoff'; Bob Grant; Blanquita Collum; Bill O'Reilly; Bill Gertz; Barry Farber; Art Bell"

I then emailed the article to even more individuals and companies, including the following:

Steven Swan

From: "Steven Swan" <stevenswan@earthlink.net>
To: "Hippo Press" <hippo@hippopress.com>; "The Hill Newspaper" <lyngling@hillnews.com>; "Barrons" <howard.gold@barrons.com>; "Boston Phoenix" <letters@phx.com>; "Investor's Business Daily" <ibdnews@investors.com>; "Jewish World Review" <schmooze@jewishworldreview.com>; "National Enquirer" <letters@nationalenquirer.com>; "Star" <letters@starmagazine.com>; "The Spotlight" <libertylobby@earthlink.net>; "The Spotlight" <thespotlight@earthlink.net>; "Beaver Cole" <bcole@longview.net>; "New England Cable News" <feedback@necn.com>; "WBZ" <newstips@wbz.com>; "WHDH-TV" <newstips@whdh.com>; "WMUR-TV" <news@wmur.com>; "WNDS TV" <wnds_tv@yahoo.com>; "New Hampshire Public Television" <roundtable@nhptv.unh.edu>; "Public Broadcasting System" <news@pbs.org>; "NBC News" <news@MSNBC.com>; "Fox News" <comments@foxnews.com>; "C-SPAN" <events@c-span.org>; "CNN News" <hln.comments@cnn.com>; "CNN Financial" <news@cnnfn.com>; "CNN Financial" <CNNfn.interact@turner.com>; "CBS News" <news@cbs.com>; "Bloomberg News" <news@bloomberg.com>; "BBC" <newsonline@bbc.co.uk>; "ABC News" <news@abcnews.go.com>; "MetroOne Networks" <john_tomlinson@metronetworks.com>; "Mike Barnicle" <barnicle@969fmtalk.com>; "Jay Severin" <ExtremeGames@969fmtalk.com>; "Howie Carr" <howiecarr@wrko.com>; "Alex Jones" <alex@infowars.com>; "Art Bell" <artbell@mindspring.com>; "Barry Farber" <Bfarber@ict.net>; "Bill O'Reilly" <boreilly@worldnetdaily.com>; "Blanquita Collum" <bqview@radioamerica.org>; "Bob Brinker" <bob@bobbrinker.com>; "Bob Grant" <bobgrant@wor710.com>; "Charlie Rose" <charlierose@pbs.org>; "Christopher Matthews" <cmatthews@sfchronicle.com>; "Chuck Harder" <charder@isgroup.net>; "Daytime Divas" <daytimedivas@wrko.com>; "Don Imus" <Imus@MSNBC.com>; "Jim Hightower" <info@jimhightower.com>; "Joan Rivers" <joanrivers@wor710.com>; "Lucianne Goldberg" <Lucianne@lucianne.com>; "Motley Fools" <webfool@fool.com>; "Peter Blute" <peterblute@wrko.com>; "Rush Limbaugh" <rush@eibnet.com>; "Sean Hannity" <hannity@foxnews.com>; "The O'Reilly Factor" <oreilly@foxnews.com>; "Todd Feinburg" <todd@tfnn.com>; "Geoff Metcalf" <gmetcalf@worldnetdaily.com>; "New Hampshire Public Radio" <smcpherson@nhpr.org>; "WBCN" <feedback@wbcn.com>; "WGIR AM" <staff@wgiram.com>; "WGIR FM" <staff@rock101wgir.com>; "WOR Radio" <news@wor710.com>; "WRKO" <rfritz@wrko.com>; "WTTK Radio 96.9" <listeners@969fmtalk.com>; "Genesis Communications Network" <midas2000@prodigy.net>; "CBS Radio" <cbsradiowebmaster@metronetworks.com>; "National Public Radio" <news@npr.org>; "Premier Radio Networks" <webmaster@premrad.com>; "Talk America Radio" <news@TalkAmerica.com>; "Talk America Radio" <staff@TalkAmerica.com>; "N.H. Center for Constitutional Studies" <chat@nhccs.org>; "Dan Meador" <DanMeador-owner@yahoogroups.com>; "FIJA" <WebForeman@fija.org>; "Howard Wilson" <stoneanarch@tds.net>; "ICE" <ice@iresist.com>; "Jail4judges" <jail4judges@mindspring.com>; "Justice Unlimited" <newland@rapidcity.com>; "Larry Becraft" <becraft@hiwaay.net>; "legalbear" <blsmyth@webaccess.net>; "Lindsey Springer" <lspringer@springer2000.org>; "Nolo Press" <cs@nolo.com>; "R.J. Tavel's Lisleaf" <Lis-LEAF@onelist.com>; "rightwaylaw" <rightwaylaw@crtf.org>; "teaparty" <teaparty@egroups.com>; "Tim Deaton" <timdeaton@yahoo.com>; "Lis-LEAF" <Lis-LEAF-owner@yahoogroups.com>; "Today's Business" <todaysbusiness@cnbc.com>; "Today Show" <today@MSNBC.com>; "Think Tank" <thinktank@pbs.org>; "The News with Brian Williams" <thenews@msnbc.com>; "The Daily Show" <thedailyshow@comedycentral.com>; "Talk of the Nation" <totn@npr.org>; "Sunday Morning" <sundays@cbsnews.com>; "Rivera Live" <rivera@cnbc.com>; "On the Media" <onthemedia@wnyc.org>; "Nova" <nova@wgbh.org>; "NBC Nightly News" <nightly@MSNBC.com>; "Morning Line" <morningline@msnbc.com>; "Morning Edition" <morning@npr.org>; "Morning Blend" <morningblend@msnbc.com>; "McLaughlin Group" <news@mclaughlin.com>; "Hard Ball" <hardball@cnbc.com>; "Frontline" <frontline@wgbh.org>; "Fresh Air" <freshair@whyy.org>; "Fox News Sunday" <foxnewssunday@foxnews.com>; "Fox News Now" <foxnewsnow@foxnews.com>; "Firing Line" <MarkNix13@aol.com>; "Dateline" <dateline@MSNBC.com>; "Crossfire" <crossfire@cnn.com>; "CBS Weekend News" <weekends@cbsnews.com>; "60 Minutes II" <60II@cbsnews.com>; "48 Hours" <48hours@cbsnews.com>; "Washington Times" <general@washtimes.com>; "Washington Post" <webnews@washpost.com>; "Wall Street Journal" <nywireroom@dowjones.com>; "USA Today" <news@usatoday.com>; "United Press International" <tips@upi.com>; "San Jose Mercury News" <letters@sjmercury.com>; "San Francisco Examiner" <news@sfexaminer.com>; "Philadelphia Inquirer" <Inquirer.Opinion@phillynews.com>; "Newsday" <news@newsday.com>; "Newsday" <lisabel@newsday.com>; "New York Times" <news@nytimes.com>; "N.Y. Post" <smarques@nypost.com>; "Minneapolis Star Tribune" <business@gw.startribune.com>; "Minneapolis Star Tribune" <metrostate@gw.startribune.com>; "Los Angeles Times" <Internal.News@latimes.com>; "Houston Chronicle" <newstips@chron.com>; "Christian Science Monitor" <grierp@csps.com>; "Chicago Tribune" <OJim43@aol.com>; "Chicago Sun Times" <webmaster@suntimes.com>; "Chicago Sun Times"

EXHIBIT 10C

10/6/03

Page 1 of 4

<news@suntimes.com>; "Boston Globe" <localnews@globe.com>; "Associated Press" <info@ap.org>; "N.Y. Daily News" <circhotline@nydailynews.com>; "Weekly Standard" <editor@weeklystandard.com>; "U.S. News and World Report" <sdillon@usnews.com>; "Time" <letters@time.com>; "The Nation" <news@TheNation.com>; "The Nation" <info@thenation.com>; "Salon Magazine" <salon@salon.com>; "Reason" <letters@reason.com>; "Newsweek" <WebEditors@newsweek.com>; "Media Bypass" <newsroom@4bypass.com>; "AntiShyster" <adask@gte.net>; "American Spectator" <correspondence@spectator.org>; "Slate" <Tpapers@aol.com>; "Forbes" <mnoer@forbes.net>; "Boston Herald" <newstips@bostonherald.com>; "Claremont Eagle Times" <etimes@cyberportal.net>; "Concord Monitor" <pbakke@cmonitor.com>; "Keene Sentinel" <news@keenesentinel.com>; "Lawrence Eagle Tribune" <crock@eagletribune.com>; "Merrimack Journal" <news@bedfordjournal.mv.com>; "Nashua Telegraph" <webeditor@telegraph-nh.com>; "Neighborhood News" <editor@yourneighborhoodnews.com>; "Portsmouth Herald" <pherald@aol.com>; "AFP France Presse" <contact@afp.com>; "AFP-US France Presse" <afp-us@afp.com>; "Canadian Broadcasting Corp." <tvnews@toronto.cbc.ca>; "CBC Radio" <assigndesk@toronto.cbc.ca>; "Der Spiegel" <news@spiegel.de>; "Irish Times" <news@irish-times.com>; "Kyodo News" <feedback-e@inet.kyodo.co.jp>; "Kyodo News" <news@home.kyodo.co.jp>; "Le Monde" <dispatch@Monde-diplomatique.fr>; "Sydney Morning Herald" <emailnews@smh.fairfax.com.au>; "The Daily Mail" <editor.it@dailymail.co.uk>; "The Daily Mail" <news@dailymail.co.uk>; "The Guardian" <neil.perry@guardian.co.uk>; "The Norway Post" <thenpn@online.no>; "The Press" <press@press.co.nz>; "The Sun" <news@the-sun.co.uk>; "The Sunday Times" <webmaster@sunday-times.co.uk>; "The Times of London" <webmaster@the-times.co.uk>; "U.K. Press Assn." <newsdesk@pa.press.net>; "Newsmax" <ruddyc@newsmax.com>; "American Freedom News" <news@americanfreedomnews.com>; "American Patriot Network" <apnmail@civil-liberties.com>; "Capitol Hill Blue" <editor@capitolhillblue.com>; "Drudge Report" <drudge@drudgereport.com>; "Free Republic" <jimrob@psnw.com>; "Frontpage Magazine" <poe@frontpagemag.com>; "Sierra Times" <editor@SierraTimes.com>; "World Net Daily" <news@worldnetdaily.com>; "Joe Sobran" <joe@sobran.com>; "Bill Gertz" <gertz@twtmail.com>; "Charley Reese" <creese@oriandosentinel.com>; "David Cay Johnston" <davidcay@nytimes.com>; "David Horowitz" <dhorowitz@frontpagemag.com>; "Joseph Farah" <jfarah@worldnetdaily.com>; "Paul Revere Society" <paulreveresociety@yahoo.com>; "Robert Schulz" <acta@capital.net>; "Sarah Foster" <sarahfoster@mindspring.com>; "Vin Suprynowicz" <Vin_Suprynowicz@lvrj.com>

Sent: Friday, October 26, 2001 7:21 PM
Subject: Are Americans the Victims of a Hoax?

What Really Happened.com
10-23-01
http://www.whatreallyhappened.com/hoax.html

ARE AMERICANS THE VICTIMS OF A HOAX?

"Hippo Press"; "The Hill Newspaper; "Barrons"; "Boston Phoenix"; "Investor's Business Daily"; "Jewish World Review"; "National Enquirer"; "Star"; "The Spotlight"; "The Spotlight"; "Beaver Cole"; "New England Cable News"; "WBZ"; "WHDH-TV" ; "WMUR-TV" ; "WNDS"; "New Hampshire Public Television"; "Public Broadcasting System"; "NBC News"; "Fox News"; "C-SPAN"; "CNN News"; "CNN Financial"; "CNN Financial"; "CBS New"; "Bloomberg News"; "BBC"; "ABC News"; "Metro One Networks"; "Mike Barnicle"; "Jay Severin"; "Howie Carr"; "Alex Jones"; "Art Bell"; "Barry Farber"; "Bill O'Reilly"; "Blanquita Collum"; "Bob Brinker"; "Bob Grant"; "Charlie Rose"; "Christopher Matthews"; "Chuck Harder"; "Daytime Divas"; "Don Imus"; "Jim Hightower"; "Joan Rivers"; "Lucianne Goldberg"; "Motley Fools"; "Peter Blute"; "Rush Limbaugh"; "Sean Hannity"; "The O'Reilly Factor"; "Todd Feinburg"; "Geoff Metcalf'"; "New Hampshire Public Radio"; "WBCN"; "WGIR AM"; "WGIR FM"; "WOR Radio", "WRKO"; "WFNK Radio"; "Genesis

Communications Network"; ,'CBS Radio"; "National Public Radio"; "Premier Radio Networks"; "Talk America Radio"; "Talk America Radio"; "N.H. Center for Constitutional Studies"; "Dan Meador"; "FIJA"; "Howard Wilson"; "ICE"; "Jail4Judges"; "Justice Unlimited"; "Larry Becraft'";- "legalbear"; "Lindsey Springer"; "Nolo Press"; "R.J. Tavel's Lisleaf'"; "rightwaylaw"; "teaparty"; "Tim Deaton"; "LisLEAF"; "Today's Business"; "Today Show"; "Think Tank"; "The News with Brian Williams"; "The Daily Show"; "Talk of the Nation"; "Sunday Morning"; "Rivera Live"; "On the Media"; "Nova"; "NBC Nightly News"; "Morning Line";"Morning Edition"; "Morning Blend"; "McLaughlin Group"; "Hard Ball"; "Frontline"; "Fresh Air"; "Fox News Sunday"; "Fox News Now"; "Firing Line"; "Dateline"; "Crossfire"; "CBS Weekend News"; "60 Minutes II"; "48 Hours"; "Washington Times"; "Washington Post"; "Wall Street Journal"; "USA Today"; "United Press International"; "San Jose Mercury News"; "San Francisco Examiner"; "Philadelphia Inquirer"; "Newsday"; "New York Times"; "N.Y. Post"; "Minneapolis Star Tribune"; "Minneapolis Star Tribune"; "Los Angeles Times"; "Houston Chronicle"; "Christian Science Monitor"; "Chicago Tribune"; "Chicago Sun Times"; "Chicago Sun Times"; <news@suntimes.com>; "Boston Globe" <localnews@globe.com>; "Associated Press"; "N.Y. Daily News"; "Weekly Standard"; "U.S. News and World Report"; "Time"; "The Nation"; "The Nation"; "Salon Magazine"; "Reason"; "Newsweek"; "Media Bypass"; "AntiShyster"; "American Spectator"; "Slate"; "Forbes"; "Boston Herald"; "Claremont Eagle Times"; "Concord Monitor"; "Keene Sentinel"; "Lawrence Eagle Tribune"; "Merrimack Journal"; "Nashua Telegraph"; "Neighborhood News"; "Portsmouth Herald"; "AFP France Presse"; "AFP-US France Presse";"Canadian Broadcasting Corp."; "GBC Radio"; "Der Spiegal"; "Irish Times"; "Kyodo News"; "Kyodo News"; "Le Monde"; "Sydney Morning Herald"; "The Daily Mail"; "The Daily Mail"; "The Guardian"; "The Norway Post"; "The Press"; "The Sun"; "The Sunday Times"; "The Times of London"; "U.K. Press Assn."; "Newsmax"; "American Freedom News"; "American Patriot Network"; "Capitol Hill Blue"; "Drudge Report"; "Free Republic"; "Frontpage Magazine"; "Sierra Times"; "World Net Daily"; "Joe Sobran"; "Bill Gertz"; "Charley Reese";"David Cay Johnston";"David

Horowitz"; "Joseph Farah"; "Paul Revere Society"; "Robert Schulz"; "Sarah Foster"; "Vin Suprynowicz"

On November 22, 2001, I emailed the following letter to the editor of the Union Leader newspaper in Manchester, New Hampshire:

Steven Swan

From: "Steven Swan" <stevenswan@earthlink.net>
To: "Union Leader" <letters@theunionleader.com>
 <letters@theunionleader.com>
Sent: Thursday, November 22, 2001 8:12 PM
Subject: Letter to the Editor

To the Editor:

We've been led to believe that Islamic Fundamentalists hijacked four planes on September 11th to be used in an attack against the United States. Will someone please tell me what kind of Islamic Fundamentalist goes out drinking and carousing with prostitutes the night before an attack of this type? Also, how could a bunch of Islamic Fundamentalists possibly have gotten access to the daily secret codes for Air Force One that day and caused President Bush to have to scramble to two secure Air Forces bases before he could return safely to Washington, D.C.? They couldn't. But the Israeli Mossad could. If you stop and think about it, Israel is obviously the greatest beneficiary of the United States being dragged into a war with Israel's enemies in the Middle East.

On November 10th, President Bush gave a speech to the United Nations General Assembly. One of the things he called for was a Palestinian state. The Israeli delegation to the U.N. boycotted Bush's speech that day. Two days later, a jetliner taking off from J.F.K. Airport in New York inexplicably fell apart killing everyone on board. Is anyone beginning to see a pattern here?

Steven A. Swan
P.O. Box 453
Auburn, NH 03032
(603) 483-5610

"To the Editor:

We've been led to believe that Islamic Fundamentalists hijacked four planes on September 11th to be used in an attack against the United States. Will someone please tell me what kind of Islamic Fundamentalist goes out drinking and carousing with prostitutes the night before an attack of this type? Also, how could a bunch of Islamic Fundamentalists possibly have gotten access to the daily secret codes for Air Force One that day, and caused President Bush to have to scramble to two secure Air Forces bases before he could return safely to Washington, D.C.? They couldn't. But the Israeli Mossad could. If you stop and think about it, Israel is obviously the greatest beneficiary of the United States being dragged into a war with Israel's enemies in the Middle East.

On November 10th, President Bush gave a speech to the United Nations General Assembly. One of the things he called for was a Palestinian state. The Israeli delegation to the U.N. boycotted Bush's speech that day. Two days later, a jetliner taking off from J.F.K. Airport in New York inexplicably fell apart killing everyone on board. Is anyone beginning to see a pattern here?

Steven A. Swan
P.O. Box 453
Auburn, NH 03032
(603) 483-5610"

    On November 29, 2001, I emailed the same letter to the editor of the Weirs Times newspaper in Weirs Beach, New Hampshire.

    On December 7, 2001, I emailed the following letter to the editor of the Union Leader newspaper. My contention was that the reason that the United States and its Coalition invaded Afghanistan was in order to be able to control the massive about of heroin and other narcotics produced there.

From:	"Steven Swan" <stevenswan@earthlink.net>
To:	"Union Leader" <letters@theunionleader.com> <letters@theunionleader.com>
Sent:	Friday, December 07, 2001 1:11 PM
Subject:	Letter to the Editor

"To the Editor:

When the war in Afganistan began, we were shown photos of Northern Alliance soldiers with a pile of heroin purportedly seized from the Taliban which was supposedly about to be destroyed. A few weeks later Robert Novak wrote in his nationally syndicated column that one group of drug traffickers in Afganistan (the Taliban) was about to be replaced by another group of drug traffickers (the Northern Alliance).

However, on November 24th, the AP reported that the ultraconservative Taliban had imposed a ban on producing heroin 3 years ago and that with the Taliban now on the run, the Afgani farmers were now planting opium poppies again in order to produce heroin.

According to the U.N. Drug Control Program, before the Taliban took over, Afganistan produced 75 percent of the world's heroin.

The War on Drugs is a farce. Ever since Vietnam, the U.S. State Department and the CIA (once headed by former President Bush) have been involved in world-wide drug trafficking as a way to earn money to fund their covert black operations. When are the American people going to wake up to the fact that the most qualified person in the country is never elected president; the puppet for the biggest bunch of criminals is?

Steven A. Swan
P.O. Box 453
Auburn, NH 03032
(603) 48305610

The war on Drugs is a farce. Ever since Vietnam, the U.S. State Department and the CIA (once headed by former president Bush) have been involved in worldwide drug trafficking as a way to earn money to fund their covert black operations. When are the American people going to wake up to the fact that the most qualified person in the country is never elected president; the puppet for the biggest bunch of criminals is?

Steven A. Swan
P.O. Box 453
Auburn, NH 03032
(603) 483-5610

On that same date, I also emailed that same letter to the editor of the Weirs Times in Weirs Beach, New Hampshire.

On December 24, 2001, I emailed the following letter to the editor of the Union Leader:

Steven Swan

From: "Steven Swan" <stevenswan@earthlink.net>
To: "Union Leader" <letters@theunionleader.com>
 <letters@theunionleader.com>
Sent: Monday, December 24, 2001 2:05 PM
Subject: Letter to the Editor

To the Editor:

Since September 11th, I have written many "Letters to the Editor" pointing out the fact that prior to that date, Israel had been taking a tremendous drubbing in the press because of its many killings of Palestinian protestors and because of the U.N. Commission on Racism's declaration that Zionism is a form racism. I have also been pointing out that Israel benefitted more than any other nation from the U.S. being dragged into a war with all of Israel's enemies and that there was no way that a bunch of Arabs would have known the secret daily codes of Air Force One that fateful day, which forced President Bush to fly to two secure military installations before he dared to fly back to Washington. A bunch of Arabs wouldn't have had access to the codes, but the Israeli Mossad surely would have via our dual-loyalist (Israel and the U.S.) CIA Director George Tenet.

Now that another President Bush has been elected, it is obvious that the war mongers of the military-industrial complex are again eager to test their latest weapons of mass murder on live human beings just as they did ten years ago under the first President Bush. Remember the Highway of Death where thousands of Iraqi soldiers were incinerated?

As of this date, none of my "Letters to the Editor" on this issue have been printed. I don't understand how the Union Leader can allow itself to be complicit in the deaths of thousands of innocent people, including those who were killed on September 11th. How many more innocent people must die before the Union Leader allows these evil Israeli terrorists to be exposed for what they really are?

Steven A. Swan
P.O. Box 453
Auburn, NH 03032
(603) 483-5610

"To the Editor:

Since September 11th, I have written many "Letters to the Editor" pointing out the fact that prior to that date, Israel had been taking a tremendous drubbing in the press because of its many killings of Palestinian protestors and because of the U.N. Commission on Racism's declaration that Zionism is a form racism. I have also been pointing out that Israel benefitted more than any other nation from the U.S. being dragged into a war with all of Israel's enemies and that there was no way that a bunch of Arabs would have known the secret daily codes for Air Force One that fateful day, which forced President Bush to fly to two secure military installations beforehe dared to fly back to Washington. A bunch of Arabs wouldn't have had access to the codes, but the Israeli Mossad surely would have via our dual-loyalist (Israel and the U.S.) CIA Director George Tenet.

Now that another President Bush has been elected, it is obvious that the war mongers of the military industrial complex are again eager to test their latest weapons of mass murder on live human beings just as they did ten years ago under the first President Bush. Remember the Highway of Death where thousands of Iraqi soldiers were incinerated?

As of this date, none of my "Letters to the Editor" on this issue have been printed. I don't understand how the Union Leader can allow itself to be complicit in the deaths of thousands of innocent people, including those who were killed on September 11th. How many more innocent people must die before the Union Leader allows these evil Israeli terrorists to be exposed for what they really are?

Steven A. Swan
P.O. Box 453

Auburn, NH 03032
(603) 483-5610"

On December 28, 2001, I emailed the following letter entitled "How Long Will the News Media Allow Itself to Be Manipulated and Duped?" to many individuals and companies:

Steven Swan

From: "Steven Swan" <stevenswan@earthlink.net>
To: "Bill Gertz" <bgertz@washingtontimes.com>; "Vin Suprynowicz" <Vin_Suprynowicz@lvrj.com>; "Joe Sobran" <joe@sobran.com>; "Charley Reese" <creese@orlandosentinel.com>; "Dan Meador" <DanMeador-owner@yahoogroups.com>; "David Cay Johnston" <davidcay@nytimes.com>; "David Horowitz" <dhorowitz@frontpagemag.com>; "Joseph Farah" <jfarah@worldnetdaily.com>; "Paul Revere Society" <paulreveresociety@yahoo.com>; "Robert Schulz" <acta@capital.net>; "Sarah Foster" <sarahfoster@mindspring.com>
Sent: Friday, December 28, 2001 6:04 PM
Subject: How Long Will the News Media Allow Itself to Be Manipulated and Duped?

For Immediate Release: December 28, 2001

Contact: Steven A. Swan

When is the news media going to wake up and realize that they have been misled by the state of Israel as to what really happened on September 11th? Or are many of them part of a grand conspiracy to cover-up Israel's complicity in the attacks upon America?

Prior to September 11th, Israel was taking a beating in the mainstream press. Ariel Sharon had purposely destabilized the region so that he could become the next Prime Minister by attending the Muslims high holy prayers in Jerusalem with 1100 heavily armed soldiers and police. The Muslims were outraged by this (as Sharon knew they would be), which lead to massive riots. For months prior to September 11th, the nightly news was full of stories about Israeli troops killing rock-throwing Palestinian youths.

Also in the news at that time were stories of how Israel and the United States had boycotted the meetings of the United Nation's Commission on Racism in Durban, South Africa because many U.N. members wanted to return to an official designation of Zionism as equating Racism, a designation it had held up until 1992. After many days of infighting at the conference, the story title in many newspapers on Saturday, September 8th was "U.N. Conference Ends in Turmoil." Israel had been receiving a lot of negative press about this.

On September 11, 2001, four airplanes were hijacked by Arab terrorists using boxcutters. Two of the planes were flown into the World Trade Center towers in New York City, one was flown into the Pentagon, and one crashed into a field in Pennsylvania. Within minutes after the attacks, the news media was stating that Osama bin Laden had orchestrated the attacks.

Now remember that Osama bin Laden had been a CIA operative prior to becoming a "rogue agent". During the 1990's he had become the latest convenient bogeyman for the administration to use whenever it needed a diversion, as Saddam Hussein had been before him and Abu Nidal had been before him and Mohammar Quaddafi had been before him. President Clinton used Osama bin Laden as a scapegoat many times, whenever Clinton needed a diversion from his numerous scandals.

Another thing happened on September 11th that the media no longer talks about. At the time of the attacks, President Bush was in Florida. After learning of the attacks, he boarded Air Force One to return to Washington. But while en route, Air Force One received word that the terrorists knew the secret daily codes for the President that day, which caused everyone, including the Secret Service, to panic. The pilot immediately flew the plane up to 40,000 feet. Then the President was diverted to two secure Air Force bases (one in the South and one in Nebraska, where he held a conference call with his advisors) before they dared to fly back to Washington.

Now, does anybody really believe that a bunch of Arab terrorists would have been able to access the secret daily codes of the President that day? Of course not. But the Israeli Mossad surely could have. Especially with a little help of dual-loyalist (Israeli-United States) CIA Director George Tenet. And who other than the state of Israel had more to gain from the United States being dragged into a war with all of Israel's enemies? Not to mention the fact that Israel desperately needed a diversion to stop all of the negative press it had been receiving as I stated earlier. But the mainstream media has conveniently forgotten all about President Bush and Air Force One having to scramble for their own safety that fateful day.

And how about President Bush's speech to the United Nations General Assembly on Saturday, November 10th in which he called for a Palestinian state. The speech was carried live on many television and radio stations. As the camera roamed around the room highlighting each country's delegates as Bush mentioned them, when he named the PLO, the camera focused on Yassar Arafat. But when Bush mentioned Israel in the same breath, the camera showed that the Israeli delegates were absent. They were boycotting Bush's speech because they are against a Palestinian state. Even many of the commentators were dumbfounded by the Israelis' absence. "Where was the Israeli delegation?" "I don't know. They must have been in the bathroom."

And just two short days later, on November 12th, American Airlines Flight 587 mysteriously fell apart on takeoff from J.F.K. International Airport in New York, killing 260 people. It must have been a coincidence, right?

EXHIBIT 16

10/6/03

As I stated earlier, Israel is by far the greatest beneficiary of the United States being drawn into a war with all of Israel's enemies. And even though I'm not sure that the Bush administration was involved in the initial attacks, they were surely quick to capitalize upon the attacks by going to war in Afganistan. What better way for the war profiteers to try out their latest weaponry on human targets, just as they did under the previous President Bush in the Persian Gulf War (Operation Desert Slaughter). Not to mention the fact that Afganistan is strategically located as an oil and natural gas pipeline route from some of the former Soviet republics to India and Pakistan.

And now the Israelis (led by dual-loyalist Deputy Secretary of Defense Paul Wolfowitz) are beating the drum to go after another one of Israel's enemies, Iraq. Who will be next? Iran, Saudi Arabia, Yemen, Syria, Jordan, Lebanon, etc.? Pretty convenient for Israel to dupe the United States into fighting its wars for it, don't you think?

Why isn't anyone in the mainstream media asking these questions and bringing up these obvious issues? Because we have been brain-washed for decades that Israel can do no wrong. And that Israelis and Jews in general must never be criticized. Not to mention the fact that there is a tremendous amount of Jewish influence in the news and entertainment media in this country.

I was watching an "American Experience" program on PBS the other night. It was the biography of Charles Lindbergh. On September 11, 1941 (sixty years to the day before the attacks on the United States), he was giving a speech in Des Moines, Iowa in which he stated "Large Jewish ownership and influence in our motion pictures, our press, our radio and our government constituted a great danger to our country." (www.pbs.org) And so it goes.

Wake up, news media. How about using a little common sense in reporting these stories and stop relying so much on handouts from the AP and the major news outlets? How about exposing these manipulators while we still have a country to save?

Steven A. Swan
P.O. Box 453
Auburn, NH 03032

"Subject: How Long Will the News Media Allow Itself to Be Manipulated and Duped?
For Immediate Release: December 28, 2001

Contact: Steven A. Swan

When is the news media going to wake up and realize that they have been misled by the state of Israel as to what really happened on September 1lth? Or are many of them part of a grand conspiracy to cover up Israel's complicity in the attacks upon America?

Prior to September 11th, Israel was taking a beating in the mainstream press. Ariel Sharon had purposely destabilized the region so that he could become the next Prime Minister by attending the Muslims high holy prayers in Jerusalem with 1100 heavily armed soldiers and police. The Muslims were outraged by this (as Sharon knew they would be), which led to massive riots. For months prior to September 11th, the nightly news was full of stories about Israeli troops killing rock throwing Palestinian youths.

Also in the news at that time were stories of how Israel and the United States had boycotted the meetings of the United Nation's Commission on Racism in Durban, South Africa because many U.N. members wanted to return to an official designation of Zionism as equating Racism, a designation it had held up until 1992. After many days of infighting at the conference, the story title in many newspapers on Saturday, September 8th was "U.N. Conference Ends in Turmoil." Israel had been receiving a lot of negative press about this.

On September 11, 2001, four airplanes were hijacked by Arab terrorists using boxcutters. Two of the planes were flown into the World Trade Center towers in New York City, one was flown into the Pentagon, and one crashed into a field in Pennsylvania. Within minutes after the attacks, the news media was stating that Osama bin Laden had orchestrated the attacks.

Now remember that Osama bin Laden had been a CIA operative prior to becoming a "rogue agent". During the 1990's he had become the latest convenient bogeyman for the administration to use whenever it needed a diversion, as Saddam Hussein had been before him and Abu Nidal had been before him and Mohammar Quaddafi had been before him. President Clinton used Osama bin Laden as a scapegoat many times, whenever Clinton needed a diversion from his numerous scandals.

Another thing happened on September 11th that the media no longer talks about. At the time of the attacks, President Bush was in Florida. After learning of the attacks, he boarded Air Force One to return to Washington. But while en route, Air Force One received word that the terrorists knew the secret daily codes for the President that day, which caused everyone, including the Secret Service, to panic. The pilot immediately flew the plane up to 40,000 feet. Then the President was diverted to two secure Air Force bases (one in the South and one in Nebraska, where he held a conference call with his advisors) before they dared to fly back to Washington.

Now, does anybody really believe that a bunch of Arab terrorists would have been able to access the secret daily codes of the President that day? Of course not. But the Israeli Mossad surely could have. Especially with a little help of dual loyalist (Israel-United States) CIA Director George Tenet. And who other than the state of Israel had more to gain from the United States being dragged into a war with all of Israel's enemies? Not to mention the fact that Israel desperately needed a diversion to stop all of the negative press it had been receiving as I stated earlier. But the mainstream media has conveniently forgotten all about President Bush and Air Force One having to scramble for their own safety that fateful day.

And how about President Bush's speech to the United Nations General Assembly on Saturday, November 10th in which he called for a Palestinian state. The speech was carried live on many television and radio stations. As the camera roamed around the room highlighting each country's delegates as Bush mentioned them, when he named the PLO, the camera focused on Yassar Arafat. But when Bush mentioned Israel in the same breath, the camera showed that the Israeli delegates were absent. They were boycotting Bush's speech because they are against a Palestinian state. Even many of the commentators were dumbfounded by the Israelis' absence. "Where was the Israeli delegation?" "I don't know. They must have been in the bathroom."

And just two short days later, on November 12th, American Airlines Flight 587 mysteriously fell apart on takeoff from J.F.K. International Airport in New York, killing 260 people. It must have been a coincidence, right?

As I stated earlier, Israel is by far the greatest beneficiary of the United States being drawn into a war with all of Israel's enemies. And even though I'm not sure that the Bush administration was involved in the initial attacks, they were surely quick to capitalize upon the attacks by going to war in Afganistan. What better way for the war profiteers to try out their latest weaponry on human targets, just as they did under the previous President Bush in the Persian Gulf War (Operation Desert Slaughter). No to mention the fact that Afganistan is strategically located as an oil and natural gas pipeline route from some of the former Soviet republics to India and Pakistan.

And now the Israelis (led by dual-loyalist Deputy Secretary of Defense Paul Wolfowitz) are beating the drum to go after another one of Israel's enemies, Iraq. Who will be next? Iran, Saudi Arabia, Yemen, Syria, Jordan, Lebanon, etc. Pretty convenient for Israel to dupe the United States into fighting its wars for it, don't you think?

Why isn't anyone in the mainstream media asking these questions and bringing up these obvious issues? Because we have been brain-washed for decades that Israel can do no wrong. And that Israelis and Jews in general must never be criticized. Not to mention the fact that there is a tremendous amount of Jewish influence in the news and entertainment media in this country.

I was watching an "American Experience" program on PBS the other night. It was the biography of Charles Lindbergh. On September 11, 1941 (sixty years to the day before the attacks on the United States), he was giving a speech in Des Moines, Iowa in which he stated "Large Jewish ownership and influence in our motion pictures, our press, our radio and our government constituted a great danger to our country." (www.pbs.org) And so it goes.

Wake up, news media. How about using a little common sense in reporting these stories and stop relying so much on handouts from the AP and the major news outlets? How about exposing these manipulators while we still have a country to save?

Steven A. Swan
P. O. Box 453
Auburn, NH 03032"

In addition to the individuals listed at the top of this email, I also sent it to the following people and entities:

"Newsmax"; "American Freedom News"; "Capitol Hill Blue", "Drudge Report", "Free Republic", "Frontpage Magazine", "Lucianne Goldberg", "Sierra Times", "World Net Daily", "AFP France Presse", "AFP-US France Presse", "BBC", "Canadian Broadcasting Corp.", "CBC Radio", "Der Spiegal", "Irish Times", " Kyodo News", "Le Monde", "Sydney Morning Herald", " The Daily Mail ", "The Daily Mail", "The Guardian", "The Norway Post", "The Press", "The Sun", "The Sunday Times", "The Times of London", "U.K. Press Assn.", "Boston Herald", "Claremont Eagle Times ", "Concord Monitor", "Keene Sentinel", "Lawrence Eagle Tribune", "Merrimack Journal", "Nashua Telegraph", "Neighborhood News", "Portsmouth Herald", "Weekly Standard", "Time", "The Nation", "Reason", "Newsweek", "Media Bypass", "AntiShyster", "Slate", "Forbes", "U.S. News and World Report", "The Nation", "Salon.com", "N.Y. Post", "USA Today", "Washington Times", "Wall Street Journal", "United Press International", "San Jose Mercury News", "San Francisco Examiner", "Philadelphia Inquirer", "Newsday", "Newsday", "New York Times", "Minneapolis Star Tribune ", "Minneapolis Star Tribune", "Investor' s Business Daily", "Houston Chronicle", "Christian Science Monitor", "Chicago Tribune", "Chicago Sun Times", "Chicago Sun Times", "Boston Globe", "Associated Press", "Washington Post", "N.Y. Daily News", "Tim Deaton", "Lindsey Springer", "legal bear", "Larry Becraft ", "Justice Unlimited", "Jail4judges", "ICE", "Howard Wilson", "FIJA", "N.H. Center for Constitutional Studies", "Today' s Business", "Today Show", "Think Tank", "The O'Reilly Factor", "The News with Brian Williams", "The Daily Show", "Talk of the Nation", "Sunday Morning", "Rivera Live", "On the Media", "Nova", "NBC Nightly News", "Morning Edition", "McLaughlin Group", "Hard Ball ", "Frontline", "Fresh Air", "Fox News Now", "Firing Line", "Dateline", "Crossfire", "CB S Weekend News", "60 Minutes II", "48 Hours", "Fox News Sunday", "Genesis Communications Network", "CBS Radio", "Metro One Networks", "Premier Radio Networks", "Talk America Radio", "Talk America Radio", "New Hampshire Public Radio", "WBCN", "WGIR AM ", "WGIR FM", "WOR Radio", "WRKO Radio, "WTTK Radio 96.9", "Mike Barnicle ", "Jay Severin", "Howie Carr", "Alex Jones", "Barry Farber", "Bill O'Reilly", "Blanquita Collum", "Bob Brinker", "Bob Grant", "Christopher Matthews", "Daytime Divas", "Don Imus", "Jim Hightower", "Joan Rivers", "Lucianne Goldberg", "Motley Fools", "Peter Blute", "Rush Limbaugh", "Sean Hannity", "The O'Reilly Factor", "Todd Feinburg", "Geoff Metcalf", "Chuck Harder", "Alfred and Melva Keithley", "Charlie Rose", "All Things Considered", "Allen Hebert", "Art Bell.Com", "Public Broadcasting System", "NBC News", "Fox News", "C-SPAN", "CNN Financial", "CNN Financial", "CBS News", "BBC ", "ABC News", "Metro One Networks", "New England Cable News", "WBZ", "WHDH-Tv.", "WMUR-Tv.", "WNDS TV", "New Hampshire Public Television", "Hippo Press", "The Hill Newspaper", "Barrons", "Boston Phoenix", "Investor's Business Daily", "Jewish World Review", "National Enquirer", "Star", "Beaver Cole", "American Free Press", "CNN Financial"; and every sitting U.S. Congressman and U.S. Senator.

On December 29, 2001, I widely distributed the following message which included a transcript of a radio address by Dr. William Pierce of the *National Alliance*. It was regarding a number of reports about Israeli espionage against the United States and other information detrimental to the Zionists having been removed from the *Fox News'* website after they had already been broadcast on national television.

That information included the fact that an Israeli company called Amdocs, Ltd. handled virtually all of the directory assistance calls and the call records and billing for virtually all of the telephone companies in the United States and the rest of the Western world; that another Israeli company called Comverse Infosys was the coordinator of nearly all of the telephone wire-tapping technology and equipment used by nearly all federal, state, and local law enforcement in the United States, including the Federal Bureau of Investigation (F.B.I.), the U.S. Drug Enforcement Agency (D.E.A.), and the U.S. Immigration and Naturalization Service (I.N.S.); that Israel conducts the most aggressive spying against the United States of any of its allies; that Israeli spies had penetrated U.S. military bases, the F.B.I., the D.E.A., dozens of Government facilities, and even the secret offices and unlisted private homes of law enforcement and military personnel; that pursuing or even suggesting that Israel was spying on the U.S. through Comverse Infosys was considered by Government investigators to be "career suicide"; that Israeli organized crime in the United States controlled virtually all of the illegal importation of the drug Ecstasy, as well as a substantial amount of cocaine smuggling, and credit card and computer fraud; that a federal, state, and local drug investigation in Los Angeles, California in 1997 into Israeli organized crime drug trafficking was compromised via the illegal use of telecommunications information handled by Amdocs, Ltd.; that a number of suspects in the investigation of the World Trade Center attack on September 11, 2001 immediately changed the way that they communicated after supposedly secret wire-taps went into effect; etc.

Steven Swan

From: "Steven Swan" <stevenswan@earthlink.net>
To: "Sarah Foster" <sarahfoster@mindspring.com>; "Robert Schulz" <acta@capital.net>; "Paul Revere Society" <paulreveresociety@yahoo.com>; "Joseph Farah" <jfarah@worldnetdaily.com>; "David Horowitz" <dhorowitz@frontpagemag.com>; "David Cay Johnston" <davidcay@nytimes.com>; "Dan Meador" <DanMeador-owner@yahoogroups.com>; "Charley Reese" <creese@orlandosentinel.com>; "Joe Sobran" <joe@sobran.com>; "Vin Suprynowicz" <Vin_Suprynowicz@lvrj.com>; "Bill Gertz" <bgertz@washingtontimes.com>; "Niel Young" <advocates@weirs.com>
Sent: Saturday, December 29, 2001 4:13 PM
Subject: Recent Fox News Stories Concerning Israeli Espionage Have Been Spiked and Removed from Fox's Web Site!

The following excerpts are with regard to a series of recent Fox News stories concerning Israeli espionage against the United States which have been spiked and removed from Fox's Web site.

Steven A. Swan

One aspect of the problem recently came to light after the September 11 attack, when the FBI began rounding up and interrogating illegal aliens who came here from Middle Eastern countries, including Israel. What the FBI uncovered is the largest espionage ring ever to operate in America.

Actually, the investigation of Israeli spying began before September 11, and many Jewish spies already had been identified. According to a Fox News report two weeks ago, as many as 140 Jewish spies already had been arrested before September 11, but there had been very little publicity about these arrests. The Bush government and most of the media were hoping no one would notice. The post-September 11 roundup of Middle Easterners uncovered another 60 or so Israelis engaged in espionage inside the United States and brought the previously secret investigation of Israeli espionage into the open -- or at least, more nearly into the open than before. The lemmings still are so busy watching their ball games that they haven't noticed.

Several very disturbing revelations have come out of this roundup. One is a very strong hint that the Jews here, through their spying on other Middle Easterners in the United States, had gained prior knowledge of the September 11 attack but did not share their information with the U.S. government. I reported my own suspicions in this regard immediately after the attack, but since then Fox News has reported even stronger suspicions among FBI investigators. A Fox News report of December 12, by reporter Carl Cameron, says, and I quote: "There is no indication the Israelis were involved in the September 11 attacks, but investigators suspect that they may have gathered intelligence about the attacks in advance and not shared it." -- end of quote --

This is the sort of thing that both the Israelis and the Bush government would like to keep quiet, and the FBI is being very tight-lipped about it now, but I will not be surprised to see the beans spilled about the Jewish foreknowledge of the attack as the investigation proceeds. The reason I say that is that the roundup of Jewish spies has revealed many other things about Israeli activities that are damaging to Americans, and it will be very difficult for the government and the media to keep everything covered up.

Here's an example: As the government has become increasingly intrusive, snooping into every aspect of our lives, the need for telephonic wiretaps and other forms of electronic surveillance has risen dramatically. You might be surprised to learn that the government doesn't do most of the electronic snooping itself; the work has become quite high-tech these days and is farmed out to private companies that specialize in electronic eavesdropping and in the storage and analysis of intercepted data. There are a number of companies, in the United States and elsewhere, that have the equipment and the expertise to do

EXHIBIT 17

this very sophisticated work. Guess which companies our government uses to spy on us: the two companies that do nearly all of this work for the Federal government are both located in Israel.

Did you get that? The politicians who run our government decided that the country that gave us Jonathan Pollard and the murderous assault on the USS Liberty is the country we should trust to help us catch our criminals and spies and keep an eye on the private business of our citizens. Really! Most state and local police agencies also depend on the same two Israeli companies.

I'll quote again directly from a Fox News report by Carl Cameron, this one dated December 13: -- quote -- "Here's how the system works. Most directory assistance calls and virtually all call records and billing in the U.S. are done for the phone companies by Amdocs, Ltd., an Israeli-based private telecommunications company. Amdocs has contracts with the 25 biggest phone companies in America, and more worldwide. The White House and other secure government phones are protected, but it is virtually impossible to make a call on normal phones without generating an Amdocs record of it. In recent years the FBI and other government agencies have investigated Amdocs more than once. The firm has repeatedly and adamantly denied any security breaches or wrongdoing. But sources tell Fox News that in 1999 the super-secret National Security Agency, headquartered in northern Maryland, issued what's called a Top Secret/Sensitive Compartmentalized Information report, TS/SCI, warning that records of calls in the United States were getting into foreign hands -- in Israel, in particular." -- end of quote --

Indeed, there has been more than one warning about the misuse of confidential communications. Law enforcement officials have reported that they are certain that their own communications have been intercepted by criminals they were investigating. They believe that the interception of their communications has led to the murder of several of their confidential informants and otherwise has hampered their investigations of illegal drug distribution by crime syndicates. And I should mention that the fastest-growing illegal drug syndicate in the United States during the past decade is the syndicate that distributes the drug known as "Ecstasy." This syndicate is entirely Jewish, and most of the Jews in the illegal distribution of "Ecstasy" in the United States are Israeli nationals. No wonder that business has been good for them!

Well, Jewish organized crime got a big boost in 1994, during the Clinton administration, with the passage of a new law, the so-called "Communications Assistance for Law Enforcement Act," or CALEA for short. What the public was told about CALEA is that it would increase public safety by providing new tools for the cops to go after the bad guys. It would centralize and expedite the business of wiretapping, making it easier for law enforcement to eavesdrop on communications between criminals -- well, to tell the truth, easier to eavesdrop on everybody. The key to CALEA was its centralizing of wiretap operations, so that now any law-enforcement official in the country who needs a wiretap knows where to go. He goes to a private company that specializes in providing wiretapping services and equipment. Now I will quote again from a Fox News report. This one was broadcast last week. I quote:

"The company is Comverse Infosys, a subsidiary of an Israeli-run private telecommunications firm, with offices throughout the U.S. It provides wiretapping equipment for law enforcement. Here's how wiretapping works in the U.S.

"Every time you make a call it passes through the nation's elaborate network of switchers and routers run by the phone companies. Custom computers and software, made by companies like Comverse, are tied into that network to intercept, record, and store the wiretapped calls and at the same time transmit them to investigators.

"The manufacturers have continuing access to the computers so they can

10/7/03

service them and keep them free of glitches. This process was authorized by the 1994 Communications Assistance for Law Enforcement Act, or CALEA. Senior government officials have now told Fox News that while CALEA made wiretapping easier, it has led to a system that is seriously vulnerable to compromise and may have undermined the whole wiretapping system. . . . [T]he complaint about this system is that the wiretap computer programs made by Comverse have, in effect, a back door through which wiretaps themselves can be intercepted by unauthorized parties.

"Adding to the suspicions is the fact that in Israel Comverse works closely with the Israeli government and under special programs gets reimbursed for up to 50 per cent of its research and development costs by the Israeli Ministry of Industry and Trade. But investigators within the DEA, INS, and FBI have all told Fox News that to pursue or even suggest Israeli spying through Comverse is considered career suicide."
-- end of quote --

Now I'll repeat just the last sentence of that quote from the December 17 Fox News report: "Investigators within the Drug Enforcement Administration, the Immigration and Naturalization Service, and the Federal Bureau of Investigation have all told Fox News that to pursue or even suggest Israeli spying through Comverse is considered career suicide." Did you get that? And the Fox News report goes on to say that every FBI inquiry into Comverse has been halted before the actual equipment could be tested for leaks.

And that's not all that's been halted. This series of Fox News reports by reporter Carl Cameron from which I have quoted was available on the Internet from the Fox News Web site through the early part of last week. The report I just quoted, which was the third in what was intended to be a four-part series, was posted on December 17. But as you can imagine our "chosen" minority did not like the series. A December 20 story from the Jewish Telegraphic Agency says, and I quote, "Jewish organizations have been receiving frantic calls from Jews concerned that the reports may fuel anti-Semitism."

Did you get that? The Fox News reports were making Jews "frantic." The Jewish Telegraphic Agency story also says, and again I quote: "American Jewish leaders and Israeli officials said they are holding conversations with Fox News representatives but refused to elaborate." -- end quote -- Well, that JTA story was from December 20, and apparently the "conversations" between Jewish leaders and Fox News were effective, because within 24 hours the Fox News series on Israeli spying was cancelled, and the three installments that already had been broadcast were yanked from the Internet and dropped into the memory hole as if they never had existed. You'll look for them in vain at the Fox News site now. The only places you'll find them are on sites that copied them from the Fox News sites before Fox News was pressured into pulling them.

To me the most interesting information in this Fox News series really is old news to a lot of people in the government and the media. The FBI and other government agencies knew what these Jewish companies, Amdocs and Comverse Infosys, were doing a long time ago. They knew that Israeli organized crime was getting information about U.S. government, business, and private telephone conversations and also about U.S. law enforcement wiretaps and was using this information for criminal purposes to the detriment of Americans. They also knew that they were supposed to pretend that they didn't know, or else: career suicide.

I'll quote one more paragraph from the December 17 Fox News report about the Israeli penetration of our wiretap system. I quote: "And what troubles investigators most, particularly in New York, in the counter-terrorism investigation of the World Trade Center attack, is that on a number of cases, suspects that they had sought to wiretap and survey immediately changed their telecommunications processes. They started acting much differently as soon as those supposedly secret wiretaps went into place." -- end of quote --

10/7/03

> It's information of this sort, hinting that the Israelis not only knew about the September 11 attack in advance but now are doing everything they can to hinder the American investigation into the attack, that the Jews don't want the American people to have. They don't want the American people to know that they have been betrayed by Israel. That is why the Fox News series was cancelled last week and the parts that already had been published were pulled from public access and tossed down the memory hole.
>
> Well, regardless of what eventually comes out about what the Israelis knew before September 11, it is clear that Israel has been engaged in an ongoing betrayal of America. What is an even greater betrayal of America than that, however, is what Attorney General John Ashcroft and George Bush and the rest of the politicians and bureaucrats in Washington have been engaged in throughout their careers.
>
> These excerpts are from Dr. William Pierce's (of the National Alliance www.natall.com) weekly address.

"Saturday, December 29, 2001 4:13 PM

Recent Fox News Stories Concerning Israeli Espionage Have Been Spiked and Removed from Fox's Web Site!

The following excerpts are with regard to a series of recent Fox News stories concerning Israeli espionage against the United States which have been spiked and removed from Fox's Web site.

Steven A. Swan

One aspect of the problem recently came to light after the September 11 attack, when the FBI began rounding up and interrogating illegal aliens who came here from Middle Eastern countries, including Israel. What the FBI uncovered is the largest espionage ring ever to operate in America.

Actually, the investigation of Israeli spying began before September 11, and many Jewish spies already had been identified. According to a Fox News report two weeks ago, as many as l40 Jewish spies already had been arrested before September 11, but there had been very 1ittle publicity about these arrests. The Bush government and most of the media were hoping no one would notice. The post-September 11 roundup of Middle Easterners uncovered another 60 or so Israelis engaged in espionage inside the

United States and brought the previously secret investigation of Israeli espionage into the open -- or at least, more nearly into the open than before. The lemmings still are so busy watching their ball games that they haven't noticed.

Several very disturbing revelations have come out of this roundup. One is a very strong hint that the Jews here, through their spying on other Middle Easterners in the United States, had gained prior knowledge of the September 11 attack but did not share their information with the U. S. government. I reported my own suspicions in this regard immediately after the attack, but since then Fox News has reported even stronger suspicions among FBI investigators. A Fox News report of December 12, by reporter Carl Cameron, says, and I quote: "There is no indication the Israelis were involved in the September 11 attacks, but investigators suspect that they may have gathered intelligence about the attacks in advance and not shared it." -- end of quote --

This is the sort of thing that both the Israelis and the Bush government would like to keep quiet, and the FBI is being very tight-lipped about it now, but I will not be surprised to see the beans spilled about the Jewish foreknowledge of the attack as the investigation proceeds. The reason I say that is that the roundup of Jewish spies has revealed many other things about Israeli activities that are damaging to Americans, and it will be very difficult for the government and the media to keep everything covered up.

Here's an example: As the government has become increasingly intrusive, snooping into every aspect of our lives, the need for telephonic wiretaps and other forms of electronic surveillance has risen dramatically. You might be surprised to learn that the government doesn't do most of the electronic snooping itself; the work has become quite high-tech these days and is farmed out to private companies that specialize in electronic eavesdropping and in the storage and analysis of intercepted data. There are a number of companies, in the United States and elsewhere, that have the equipment and the expertise to do this very sophisticated work. Guess which companies our government uses to spy on us: the two companies that do nearly all of this work for the federal government are both located in Israel.

Did you get that? The politicians who run our government decided that the country that gave us Jonathan Pollard and the murderous assault on the USS Liberty is the country we should trust to help us catch our criminals and spies and keep an eye on the private business of our citizens. Really! Most state and local police agencies also depend on the same two Israeli companies.

I'll quote again directly from a Fox News report by Carl Cameron, this one dated December 13: -- quote -- "Here's how the system works. Most directory assistance calls and virtually all call records and billing in the U.S. are done for the phone companies by Amdocs, Ltd., an Israeli-based private telecommunications company. Amdocs has contracts with the 25 biggest phone companies in America, and more worldwide. The White House and other secure government phones are protected, but it is virtually impossible to make a call on normal phones without generating an Amdocs record of it, In recent years the FBI and other government agencies have investigated Amdocs more than once. The firm has repeatedly and adamantly denied any security breaches or wrongdoing. But sources tell Fox News that in 1999 the super-secret National Security Agency, headquartered in northern Maryland, issued what's called a Top Secret/Sensitive Compartmentalized Information report, TS/SCI, warning that records of calls in the United States were getting into foreign hands -- in Israel, in particular," -- end of quote --

Indeed, there has been more than one warning about the misuse of confidential communications. Law enforcement officials have reported that they are certain that their own communications have been intercepted by criminals they were investigating. They believe that the interception of their communications has led to the murder of several of their confidential informants and otherwise has hampered their investigations of illegal drug distribution by crime syndicates. And I should mention that the fastest-growing illegal drug syndicate in the United States during the past decade is the syndicate that distributes the drug known as "Ecstasy." This syndicate is entirely Jewish, and most of the Jews in the illegal distribution of "Ecstasy" in the United States are Israeli nationals. No wonder that business has been good for them!

Well, Jewish organized crime got a big boost in 1994, during the Clinton administration, with the passage of a new law, the so-called "Communications Assistance for Law Enforcement Act," or CALEA for short. What the public was told about CALEA is that it would increase public safety by providing new tools for the cops to go after the bad guys. It would centralize and expedite the business of wiretapping, making it easier for law enforcement to eavesdrop on communications between criminals -- well, to tell the truth, easier to eavesdrop on everybody. The key to CALEA was its centralizing of wiretap operations, so that now any law-enforcement official in the country who needs a wiretap knows where to go. He goes to a private company that specializes in providing wiretapping services and equipment. Now I will quote again from a Fox News report. This one was broadcast last week. I quote:

"The company is Comverse Infosys, a subsidiary of an Israeli-run private telecommunications firm, with offices throughout the U.S. It provides wiretapping equipment for law enforcement. Here's how wiretapping works in the U.S.

"Every time you make a call it passes through the nation's elaborate network of switchers and routers run by the phone companies. Custom computers and software, made by companies like Comverse, are tied into that network to intercept, record, and store the wiretapped calls and at the same time transmit them to investigators.

"The manufacturers have continuing access to the computers so they can service them and keep them free of glitches. This process was authorized by the 1994 Communications Assistance for Law Enforcement Act, or CALEA. Senior government officials have now told Fox News that while CALEA made wiretapping easier, it has led to a system that is seriously vulnerable to compromise and may have undermined the whole wiretapping system. . . . [T]he complaint about this system is that the wiretap computer programs made by Comverse have, in effect, a back door through which wiretaps themselves can be intercepted by unauthorized parties.

"Adding to the suspicions is the fact that in Israel Comverse works closely with the Israeli government and under special programs gets reimbursed for up to 50 per cent of its research and development costs by the Israeli Ministry of Industry and Trade. But investigators within the DEA, INS, and FBI have all told Fox News that to pursue or even suggest Israeli spying through Comverse is considered career suicide."

-- end of quote --

Now I'll repeat just the last sentence of that quote from the December 17 Fox News report: "Investigators within the

Drug Enforcement Administration, the Immigration and Naturalization Service, and the Federal Bureau of Investigation have all told Fox News that to pursue or even suggest Israeli spying through Comverse is considered career suicide." Did you get that? And the Fox News report goes on to say that every FBI inquiry into Comverse has been halted before the actual equipment could be tested for leaks.

And that's not all that's been halted. This series of Fox News reports by reporter Carl Cameron from which I have quoted was available on the Internet from the Fox News Web site through the early part of last week. The report I just quoted, which was the third in what was intended to be a four-part series, was posted on December 17. But as you can imagine our "chosen" minority did not like the series. A December 20 story from the Jewish Telegraphic Agency says, and I quote, "Jewish organizations have been receiving frantic calls from Jews concerned that the reports may fuel anti-Semitism."

Did you get that? The Fox News reports were making Jews "frantic." The Jewish Telegraphic Agency story also says, and again I quote: "American Jewish leaders and Israeli officials said they are holding conversations with Fox News representatives but refused to elaborate." -- end quote -- Well, that JTA story was from December 20, and apparently the "conversations" between Jewish leaders and Fox News were effective, because within 24 hours the Fox News series on Israeli spying was cancelled, and the three installments that already had been broadcast were yanked from the Internet and dropped into the memory hole as if they never had existed. You'll look for them in vain at the Fox News site now. The only places you'll find them are on sites that copied them from the Fox News sites before Fox News was pressured into pulling them.

To me the most interesting information in this Fox News series really is old news to a lot of people in the government and the media. The FBI and other government agencies knew what these Jewish companies, Amdocs and Comverse Infosys, were doing a long time ago. They knew that Israeli organized crime was getting information about U.S. government, business, and private telephone conversations and also about U.S. law enforcement wiretaps and was using this information for criminal purposes to the detriment of Americans, They also knew that they were supposed to pretend that they didn't know, or else: career suicide.

I'll quote one more paragraph from the December 17 Fox News report about the Israeli penetration of our wiretap system. I quote: "And what troubles investigators most, particularly in New York, in the counter-terrorism investigation of the World Trade Center attack, is that on a number of cases, suspects that they had sought to wiretap and survey immediately changed their telecommunications processes. They started acting much differently as soon as those supposedly secret wiretaps went into place." -- end of quote –

It's information of this sort, hinting that the Israelis not only knew about the September 11 attack in advance but now are doing everything they can to hinder the American investigation into the attack, that the Jews don't want the American people to have. They don't want the American people to know that they have been betrayed by Israel. That is why the Fox News series was cancelled last week and the parts that already been published were pulled from public access and tossed down the memory hole.

Well, regardless of what eventually comes out about what the Israelis knew before September 11, it is clear that Israel has been engaged in an ongoing betrayal of America. What is an even greater betrayal of America than that, however, is what Attorney General John Ashcroft and George Bush and the rest of the politicians and bureaucrats in Washington have been engaged in throughout their careers.

These excerpts are from Dr. William Pierce's (of the National Alliance www.natall.com) weekly address."

In addition to the individuals listed at the top of this email, I also emailed this address to the following individuals and entities:

"World Net Daily", "Sierra Times", "Lucianne Goldberg", "Frontpage Magazine", "Free Republic", "Drudge Report", "Capitol Hill Blue", "American Freedom News", "Newsmax", "AFP France Presse", "AFP-US France Presse", "BBC", "Canadian Broadcasting Corp.", "CBC Radio", "Der Spiegal", "Irish Times", "Kyodo News","Le Monde", "Sydney Morning Herald", "The Daily Mail", "The Daily Mail", "The Guardian", "The Norway Post", "The Press", "The Sun", "The Sunday Times", "The Times of London", "U.K. Press Assn.", "Boston Herald", "Claremont Eagle Times", "Concord Monitor", "Keene Sentinel", "Lawrence Eagle Tribune", "Merrimack Journal", "Nashua Telegraph", "Neighborhood News", "Portsmouth Herald", "Weekly Standard", "Time", "The Nation", "Reason", "Newsweek", "Media Bypass", "AntiShyster", "Slate", "Forbes", "U.S. News and World Report", "The Nation", "Salon.com", "N.Y. Daily News", "Washington Post", "Boston Globe", "Chicago Sun Times", "Chicago Sun Times", "Chicago Tribune", "Christian Science Monitor", "Houston Chronicle", "Investor's Business Daily", "Minneapolis Star Tribune", "Minneapolis Star Tribune", "New York Times", "Newsday", "Newsday", "Philadelphia Inquirer", "San Francisco Examiner", "San Jose Mercury News", "Wall Street Journal", "Washington Times", "USA Today", "N.Y. Post", "Associated Press", "Associated Press", "United Press International", "Reuters", "Today' s Business ", "Today Show", "Think Tank", "The O'Reilly Factor", "The News with Brian Williams", "The Daily Show", "Talk of the Nation", "Sunday Morning", "Rivera Live", "On the Media", "Nova", "NB C Nightly News", "Morning Edition", "McLaughlin

Group", "Hard Ball", "Frontline", "Fresh Air", "Fox News Now", "Firing Line", "Dateline", "Crossfire", "CBS Weekend News", "60 Minutes II", "48 Hours", "Fox News Sunday", "Liberty committee", "Tim Deaton", "Lindsey Springer", "legalbear", "Larry Becraft ", "Justice Unlimited", "Jail4judges", "ICE", "Howard Wilson", "FIJA", "N.H. Center for Constitutional Studies", "Judicial Watch", "CBS Radio", "Metro One Networks", "Premier Radio Networks", "Talk America Radio ", "Talk America Radio", "New Hampshire Public Radio", "WBCN ", "WGIR AM", "WGIR FM", "WOR Radio", "WRKO Radio", "WTTK Radio 96.9", "Art Bell.Com", "Allen Hebert", "All Things Considered", "Charlie Rose", "Alfred and Melva Keithley", "Chuck Harder", "Geoff Metcalf", "Todd Feinburg", "The O'Reilly Factor", "Sean Hannity", "Rush Limbaugh", "Peter Blute", "Motley Fools", "Lucianne Goldberg", "Joan Rivers", "Jim Hightower", "Don Imus", "Daytime Divas", "Christopher Matthews", "Bob Grant", "Bob Brinker", "Blanquita Collum", "Bill O'Reilly", "Barry Farber", "Alex Jones", "Howie Carr", "Jay Severin", "Mike Barnicle", " Public Broadcasting System", "NBC News", "Fox News", "C-SPAN", "CNN Financial", "CNN Financial", "CBS News", "BB BBC", "ABC News", "Metro One Networks", "CNN", "New England Cable News", "WBZ ", "WHDH-TV", "WMUR-TV.", "WNDS TV", "New Hampshire Public Television", "New England Cable News", "WBZ ", "WHDH-TV", "WMUR-TV.", "WNDS TV", "New Hampshire Public Television", "Hippo Press", "The Hill Newspaper", "Barrons", "Boston Phoenix", "Investor's Business Daily", "Jewish World Review", "National Enquirer", "Star", "Beaver Cole", "American Free Press", every sitting U.S. Congressman, and every sitting U.S. Senator.

On December 30, 2001, after finding copies of the news stories damaging to Israelis that *Fox News* expunged from its website, I widely distributed the links to them via email. Here is the message that I sent:

"Sent: Sunday, December 30, 2001 8:17 PM

Subject: Fox News Stories About Israeli Espionage Against the U.S. Which Have Been Spiked and Removed from Fox's Web Site

These are the links to copies of the Fox News stories about Israeli espionage against the United States which have been spiked and removed from the Fox News Web site.

Part 1 http://www.freerepublic.com/focus/fr/589762/posts

P art 2 http://www.freerepublic.com/focus/fr/590068/posts

Part 3 http://www.freerepublic.com/focus/fr/590668/posts

P art 4 http://www.freerepublic.com/focus/fr/592499/posts

Steven A. Swan"

　　　　In addition to the individuals and entities listed at the top of this email, I also emailed it to the following individuals and entities:

"Hippo Press"; "The Hill Newspaper"; "Barrons"; "Boston Phoenix"; "Investor's Business Daily"; "Jewish World Review"; "National Enquirer", "Star"; "Beaver Cole";

"American Free Press"; "World Net Daily", "Sierra Times", "Lucianne Goldberg", "Frontpage Magazine", "Free Republic", "Drudge Report", "Capitol Hill Blue", "American Freedom News", "Newsmax"; "AFP France Presse", "AFP-US France Presse", "BBC", "Canadian Broadcasting Corp. ", "CBC Radio", "Der Spiegal", "Irish Times", "Kyodo News", "Le Monde", "Sydney Morning Herald", "The Daily Mail ", "The Daily Mail", "The Guardian", "The Norway Post", "The Press", "The Sun", "The Sunday Times ", "The Times of London", "U.K. Press Assn."; " Boston Herald", "Claremont Eagle Times ", "Concord Monitor", "Keene Sentinel", "Lawrence Eagle Tribune", "Merrimack Journal", "Nashua Telegraph", "Neighborhood News", "Portsmouth Herald"; "Weekly Standard", "Time", "The Nation", "Reason", "Newsweek", "Media Bypass", "AntiShyster", "Slate", "Forbes", "U.S. News and World Report", "The Nation", "Salon.com", "Oil Patch News"; "N.Y. Daily News", "Washington Post", "Boston Globe", "Chicago Sun Times", "Chicago Sun Times ", "Chicago Tribune", "Christian Science Monitor", "Houston Chronicle", "Investor's Business Daily ", "Minneapolis Star Tribune", "Minneapolis Star Tribune ", "New York Times", "Newsday", "Newsday", "Philadelphia Inquirer", "San Francisco Examiner", "San Jose Mercury News", "Wall Street Journal", "Washington Times", "USA Today", "N.Y. Post"; "Associated Press", "Associated Press", "United Press International"; "Reuters"; "Today's Business", "Today Show", "Think Tank", "The O'Reilly Factor", "The News with Brian Williams", "The Daily Show", "Talk of the Nation"; "Sunday Morning", "Rivera Live", "On the Media", "Nova", "NBC Nightly News", "Morning Edition", "McLaughlin Group", "Hard Ball", "Frontline", "Fresh Air", "Fox News Now", "Firing Line", "Dateline", "Crossfire", "CBS Weekend News", "60 Minutes II", "48 Hours", "Fox News Sunday"; "Liberty Committee", "Tim Deaton", "Lindsey Springer", "legalbear", "Larry Becraft", "Justice Unlimited", "Jail4judges", "ICE", "Howard Wilson", "FIJA"; "N.H. Center for Constitutional Studies", "Judicial Watch"; "CBS Radio", "Metro One Networks", "Premier Radio Networks", "Talk America Radio ", "Talk America Radio"; "New Hampshire Public Radio", "WBCN", "WGIR AM", "WGIR FM", "WOR Radio", "WRKO", "WTTK Radio 96.9"; "Public Broadcasting System", "NBC News", "Fox News", "C-SPAN", "CNN Financial", "CNN Financial",

"BBC", "ABC News", "Metro One Networks", " CNN"; "Mike Barnicle"; "Jay Severin", "Howie Car", "Alex Jones", "Barry Farber", "Bill O'Reilly", "Blanquita Collum", "Bob Brinker", "Bob Grant", "Christopher Matthews", "Daytime Divas", "Don Imus", "Jim Hightower", "Joan Rivers", "Lucianne Goldberg", "Motley Fools", "Peter Blute", "Rush Limbaugh", "Sean Hannity", "The O'Reilly Factor", "Todd Feinburg", "Geoff Metcalf ", "Chuck Harder", "Alfred and Melva Keithley", "Charlie Rose", "All Things Considered", "Allen Hebert", "Art Bell.Com", "Mike Ball"; "New England Cable News", "WHDH-Tv.", "WMUR-Tv.", "WNDS TV", "New Hampshire Public Television".

The following are the *Fox News* stories that *Fox News* expunged from its website. They were posted on the *Free Republic* website-FreeRepublic.com. Here is the first one: (It erroneously states that it is the "second of four parts. Rather, it is the first of four parts.)

Carl Cameron Reports - Some U.S. investigators believe that Israel is spying in and on the..

FreeRepublic.com *"A Conservative News Forum"*

[Threads | Comments | Self-Search | Search | Topics / Post | Bookmark | Abuse | Settings | Help!]

Disclaimer: Opinions posted on Free Republic are those of the individual posters and do not necessarily represent the opinion of Free Republic or its management. All materials posted herein are protected by copyright law and the exemption for fair use of copyrighted works.

Carl Cameron Reports - Some U.S. investigators believe that Israel is spying in and on the U.S. and

Crime/Corruption
Source: foxnews
Published: **12/12/01** Author: **Carl Cameron**
Posted on **12/13/01 6:18 AM Pacific** by **Phil V.**

Carl Cameron Reports - Some U.S. investigators believe that Israel is spying in and on the U.S. and may have known things they didn't tell us before September 11

Wednesday, December 12, 2001
(second of four part series)

BRIT HUME, HOST: It has been more than 16 years since a civilian working for the Navy was charged with passing secrets to Israel. Jonathan Pollard pled guilty to conspiracy to commit espionage and is serving a life sentence. At first, Israeli leaders claimed Pollard was part of a rogue operation, but later took responsibility for his work.

Now Fox News has learned some U.S. investigators believe that there are Israelis again very much engaged in spying in and on the U.S., who may have known things they didn't tell us before September 11. Fox News correspondent Carl Cameron has details in the first of a four-part series.

(BEGIN VIDEOTAPE)

CARL CAMERON, FOX NEWS CORRESPONDENT: Since September 11, more than 60 Israelis have been arrested or detained, either under the new patriot anti-terrorism law, or for immigration violations. A handful of active Israeli military were among those detained, according to investigators, who say some of the detainees also failed polygraph questions when asked about alleged surveillance activities against and in the United States.

There is no indication that the Israelis were involved in the 9-11 attacks, but investigators suspect that they Israelis may have gathered intelligence about the attacks in advance, and not shared it. A highly placed investigator said there are "tie-ins." But when asked for details, he flatly refused to describe them, saying, "evidence linking these Israelis to 9-11 is classified. I cannot tell you about evidence that has been gathered. It's classified information."

EXHIBIT 19

http://www.freerepublic.com/focus/fr/589762/posts   12/30/01

Fox News has learned that one group of Israelis, spotted in North Carolina recently, is suspected of keeping an apartment in California to spy on a group of Arabs who the United States is also investigating for links to terrorism. Numerous classified documents obtained by Fox News indicate that even prior to September 11, as many as 140 other Israelis had been detained or arrested in a secretive and sprawling investigation into suspected espionage by Israelis in the United States.

Investigators from numerous government agencies are part of a working group that's been compiling evidence since the mid '90s. These documents detail hundreds of incidents in cities and towns across the country that investigators say, "may well be an organized intelligence gathering activity."

The first part of the investigation focuses on Israelis who say they are art students from the University of Jerusalem and Bazala Academy. They repeatedly made contact with U.S. government personnel, the report says, by saying they wanted to sell cheap art or handiwork.

Documents say they, "targeted and penetrated military bases." The DEA, FBI and dozens of government facilities, and even secret offices and unlisted private homes of law enforcement and intelligence personnel. The majority of those questioned, "stated they served in military intelligence, electronic surveillance intercept and or explosive ordinance units."

Another part of the investigation has resulted in the detention and arrests of dozens of Israelis at American mall kiosks, where they've been selling toys called Puzzle Car and Zoom Copter. Investigators suspect a front.

Shortly after The New York Times and Washington Post reported the Israeli detentions last months, the carts began vanishing. Zoom Copter's Web page says, "We are aware of the situation caused by thousands of mall carts being closed at the last minute. This in no way reflects the quality of the toy or its salability. The problem lies in the operators' business policies."

Why would Israelis spy in and on the U.S.? A general accounting office investigation referred to Israel as country A and said, "According to a U.S. intelligence agency, the government of country A conducts the most aggressive espionage operations against the U.S. of any U.S. ally."

A defense intelligence report said Israel has a voracious appetite for information and said, "the Israelis are motivated by strong survival instincts which dictate every possible facet of their political and economical policies. It aggressively collects military and industrial technology and the U.S. is a high priority target."

The document concludes: "Israel possesses the resources and technical capability to achieve its collection objectives."

(END VIDEO CLIP)

A spokesman for the Israeli embassy here in Washington issued a denial saying that any suggestion that Israelis are spying in or on the U.S. is "simply not true." There are other things to consider. And in the days ahead, we'll take a look at the U.S. phone system and law enforcement's methods for wiretaps. And an investigation that both have been compromised by our friends overseas.

HUME: Carl, what about this question of advanced knowledge of what was going to happen on 9-11? How clear are investigators that some Israeli agents may have known something?

CAMERON: It's very explosive information, obviously, and there's a great deal of evidence that they say they have collected— none of it necessarily conclusive. It's more when they put it all together. A bigger question, they say, is how could they not have known? Almost a direct quote.

HUME: Going into the fact that they were spying on some Arabs, right?

CAMERON: Correct.

HUME: All right, Carl, thanks very much.

(Messages from members of Free Republic listed at the end of this post have been removed.)

"Carl Cameron Reports - Some U.S. investigators believe that Israel is spying in and on the.. Page 1 of 6

FreeRepublic.com "A Conservative News Forum"

[Threads-Comments-Self-Search-Search-Topics-Post-Bookmark-Abuse-Settings-Help!]

Disclaimer: Opinions posted on Free Republic are those of the individual posters and do not necessarily represent the opinion of Free Republic or its management. All materials posted herein are protected by copyright law and the exemption for fair use of copyrighted works.

Carl Cameron Reports - Some U.S. investigators believe that Israel is spying in and on the U.S. and

Crime/Corruption
Source: Foxnews
Published: 12/12/01 Author: Carl Cameron
Posted on l2/l3/0l 6:18 AM Pacific by Phil v.
Carl Cameron Reports - Some U.S. investigators believe that Israel is spying in and on the U.S. and may have known things they didn't tell us before September 11

Wednesday, December 12, 2001
(second of four part series)(sic)

BRIT HUME, HOST: It has been more than 16 years since a civilian working for the Navy was charged with passing secrets to Israel. Jonathan Pollard pled guilty to conspiracy to commit espionage and is serving a life sentence. At first, Israeli leaders claimed Pollard was part of a rogue operation, but later took responsibility for his work.

Now Fox News has learned some U.S. investigators believe that there are Israelis again very much engaged in spying in and on the U.S., who may have known things they didn't tell us before September 11. Fox News correspondent Carl Cameron has details in the first of a four-part series.

(BEGIN VIDEOTAPE)

CARL CAMERON, FOX NEWS CORRESPONDENT: Since September 11, more than 60 Israelis have been arrested or detained, either under the new patriot anti-terrorism law, or for immigration violations. A handful of active Israeli military were among those detained, according to investigators, who say some of the detainees also failed polygraph questions when asked about alleged surveillance activities against and in the United States.

There is no indication that the Israelis were involved in the 9-11 attacks, but investigators suspect that they Israelis may have gathered intelligence about the attacks in advance, and not shared it. A highly placed investigator said there are "tie-ins." But when asked for details, he flatly refused to describe them, saying, "evidence linking these Israelis to 9-11 is classified. I cannot tell you about evidence that has been gathered. It's classified information."

Fox News has learned that one group of Israelis, spotted in North Carolina recently, is suspected of keeping an apartment in California to spy on a group of Arabs who the

United States is also investigating for links to terrorism. Numerous classifies documents obtained by Fox indicate that even prior to September 11, as many as 140 other Israelis had been detained or arrested in a secretive and sprawling investigation into suspected espionage by Israelis in the United States.

Investigators from numerous government agencies are part of a working group that's been compiling evidence since the mid '90s. These documents detail hundreds of incidents in cities and towns across the county that investigators say, "may well be an organized intelligence gathering activity."

The first part of the investigation focuses on Israelis who say they are art students from the University of Jerusalem and Bazala Academy. They repeatedly made contact with U.S. government personnel, the report says, by saying they wanted to sell cheap art or handiwork.

Documents say they, "targeted and penetrated military bases." The DEA, FBI and dozens of government facilities, and even secret offices and unlisted private homes of law enforcement and intelligence personnel. The majority of those questioned, "stated they served in military intelligence, electronic surveillance intercept and or explosive ordinance units."

Another part of the investigation has resulted in the detention and arrests of dozens of Israelis at American mall kiosks, where they've been selling toys called Puzzle Car and Zoom Copter. Investigators suspect a front.

Shortly after The New York Times and Washington Post reported the Israeli detentions last months, the carts began vanishing. Zoom Copter's Web page says, "We are aware of the situation caused by thousands of mall carts being closed at the last minute. This in no way reflects the quality of the toy or its saleability. The problem lies in the operators' business policies."

Why would Israelis spy in and on the U.S.? A general accounting office investigation referred to Israel as country A and said, "According to a U.S. intelligence agency, the government of country A conducts the most aggressive espionage operations against the U.S. of any U.S. ally."

A defense intelligence report said Israel has a voracious appetite for information and said, "the Israelis are motivated by strong survival instincts which dictate every possible facet of their political and economical policies. It aggressively collects military and industrial technology and the U.S. is a high priority target."

The document concludes: "Israel possesses the resources and technical capability to achieve its collection objectives."

(END VIDEO CLIP)

A spokesman for the Israeli embassy here in Washington issued a denial saying that any suggestion that Israelis are spying in or on the U.S. is "simply not true." There are other things to consider. And in the days ahead, we'll take a look at the U.S. phone system and law enforcement's methods for wiretaps. And an investigation that both have been compromised by our friends overseas.

HUME: Carl, what about this question of advanced knowledge of what was going to happen on 9-1 1? How clear are investigators that some Israeli agents may have known something?

CAMERON: It's very explosive information, obviously, and there's a great deal of evidence that they say they have collected- none of it necessarily conclusive. It's more when they put it all together. A bigger question, they say, is how could they not have know? Almost a direct quote.

HUME: Going into the fact that they were spying on some Arabs, right?

CAMERON: Correct.

HUME: All right, Carl, thanks very much."

Here is a copy of the second installment of the *Fox News* reports as posted on the *Free Republic* website-FreeRepublic.com:

Carl Cameron Investigates Part 2 - Israel Is Spying In And On The U.S.?

FreeRepublic.com *"A Conservative News Forum"*

[Threads | Comments | Self-Search | Search | Topics / Post | Bookmark | Abuse | Settings | Help!]

Disclaimer: Opinions posted on Free Republic are those of the individual posters and do not necessarily represent the opinion of Free Republic or its management. All materials posted herein are protected by copyright law and the exemption for fair use of copyrighted works.

Carl Cameron Investigates Part 2 - Israel Is Spying In And On The U.S.?

Foreign Affairs
Source: Fox New
Posted on 12/13/01 3:47 PM Pacific by RCW2001

Carl Cameron Investigates Part 2 Thursday, December 13, 2001

This partial transcript of *Special Report with Brit Hume*, Dec. 12, was provided by the Federal Document Clearing House. Click here to order the complete transcript.

Part 2 of 4

BRIT HUME, HOST: Last time we reported on the approximately 60 Israelis who had been detained in connection with the Sept. 11 terrorism investigation. Carl Cameron reported that U.S. investigators suspect that some of these Israelis were spying on Arabs in this country, and may have turned up information on the planned terrorist attacks back in September that was not passed on.

FNC

Carl Cameron   Tonight, in the second of four reports on spying by Israelis in the U.S., we learn about an Israeli-based private communications company, for whom a half-dozen of those 60 detained suspects worked. American investigators fear information generated by this firm may have fallen into the wrong hands and had the effect of impeded the Sept. 11 terror inquiry. Here's Carl Cameron's second report.

(BEGIN VIDEOTAPE)

CARL CAMERON, FOX NEWS CORRESPONDENT (voice-over): Fox News has learned that some American terrorist investigators fear certain suspects in the Sept. 11 attacks may have managed to stay ahead of them, by knowing who and when investigators are calling on the telephone. How?

By obtaining and analyzing data that's generated every time someone in the U.S. makes a call.

UNIDENTIFIED FEMALE: What city and state, please?

CAMERON: Here's how the system works. Most directory assistance calls, and virtually all call records and billing in the U.S. are done for the phone companies by Amdocs Ltd., an Israeli-based private elecommunications company.

Amdocs has contracts with the 25 biggest phone companies in America, and more worldwide. The White House and other secure government phone lines are protected, but it is virtually impossible to make a call on normal phones without generating an Amdocs record of it.

In recent years, the FBI and other government agencies have investigated Amdocs more than once. The firm has repeatedly and adamantly denied any security breaches or wrongdoing. But sources tell Fox News that in 1999, the super secret national security agency, headquartered in northern Maryland, issued what's called a Top Secret sensitive compartmentalized information report, TS/SCI, warning that records of calls in the United States were getting into foreign hands-- in Israel, in particular.

Investigators don't believe calls are being listened to, but the data about who is calling whom and when is plenty valuable in itself. An internal Amdocs memo to senior company executives suggests just how Amdocs generated call records could be used. "Widespread data mining techniques and algorithms.... combining both the properties of the customer (e.g., credit rating) and properties of the specific 'behavior....'" Specific behavior, such as who the customers are calling.

The Amdocs memo says the system should be used to prevent phone fraud. But U.S. counterintelligence analysts say it could also be used to spy through the phone system. Fox News has learned that the N.S.A has held numerous classified conferences to warn the F.B.I. and C.I.A. how Amdocs records could be used. At one NSA briefing, a diagram by the Argon national lab was used to show that if the phone records are not secure, major security breaches are possible.

Another briefing document said, "It has become increasingly apparent that systems and networks are vulnerable...Such crimes always involve unauthorized persons, or persons who exceed their authorization...citing on exploitable vulnerabilities."

Those vulnerabilities are growing, because according to another briefing, the U.S. relies too much on foreign companies like Amdocs for high-tech equipment and software. "Many factors have led to increased dependence on code developed overseas.... We buy rather than train or develop solutions."

U.S. intelligence does not believe the Israeli government is involved in a misuse of information, and Amdocs insists that its data is secure. What U.S. government officials are worried about, however, is the possibility that Amdocs data could get into the wrong hands, particularly organized crime. And that would not be the first thing that such a thing has happened. Fox News has documents of a 1997 drug trafficking case in Los Angeles, in which telephone information, the type that Amdocs collects, was used to "completely compromise the communications of the FBI, the Secret Service, the DEO and the LAPD."

We'll have that and a lot more in the days ahead – Brit.

HUME: Carl, I want to take you back to your report last night on those 60 Israelis who were detained in the antiterror investigation, and the suspicion that some investigators have that they may have picked up information on the 9/11 attacks ahead of time and not passed it on.

There was a report, you'll recall, that the Mossad, the Israeli intelligence agency, did indeed send representatives to the U.S. to warn, just before 9/11, that a major terrorist attack was imminent. How does that leave room for the lack of a warning?

CAMERON: I remember the report, Brit. We did it first internationally right here on your show on the 14th. What investigators are saying is that that warning from the Mossad was nonspecific and general, and they believe that it may have had something to do with the desire to protect what are called sources and methods in the intelligence community. The suspicion being, perhaps those sources and methods were taking place right here in the United States.

The question came up in select intelligence committee on Capitol Hill today. They intend to look into what we reported last night, and specifically that possibility – Brit.

HUME: So in other words, the problem wasn't lack of a warning, the problem was lack of useful details?

CAMERON: Quantity of information.

HUME: All right, Carl, thank you very much.

(Messages from members of Free Republic listed at the end of this post have been removed.)

"Carl Cameron Investigates Part 2 - Israel Is Spying In And On The U.S.?
Foreign Affairs
Source: For New
Posted on 12/13/01 3:47 PM Pacific by RCW2001

Carl Cameron Investigates Part 2 Thursday, December 13, 2001

This partial transcript of Special Report with Brit Hume, Dec. 12, was provided by the Federal
Document Clearing House. Click here to order the complete transcript.
Part 2 of 4

BRIT HUME, HOST: Last time we reported on the approximately 60 Israelis who had been detained in connection with the Sept. 1l terrorism investigation. Carl Cameron reported that U.S. investigators suspect that some of these Israelis were spying on Arabs in this country, and may have turned up information on the planned terrorist attacks back in September that was not passed on.

Tonight, in the second of four reports on spying by Israelis in the U.S., we learn about an Israeli-based private communications company, for whom a half dozen of those 60 detained suspects worked. American investigators fear information generated by this firm may have fallen into the wrong hands and had the effect of impeded the Sept. 1l terror inquiry. Here's Carl Cameron's second report.

(BEGIN VIDEOTAPE)

CARL CAMERON, FOX NEWS CORRESPONDENT (voice-over): Fox News has learned that some American terrorist investigators fear certain suspects in the Sept. l1 attacks may have managed to stay ahead of them, by knowing who and when investigators are calling on the telephone. How?

By obtaining and analyzing data that's generated every time someone in the U.S. makes a call.

UNIDENTIFIED FEMALE: What city and state, please?

CAMERON: Here's how the system works. Most directory assistance calls, and virtually all call records and billing in the U.S. are done for the phone companies by Amdocs Ltd., an Israeli based private telecommunications company.

Amdocs has contracts with the 25 biggest phone companies in America, and more worldwide. The White House and other secure government phone lines are protected, but it is virtually impossible to make a call on normal phones without generating an Amdocs record of it.

In recent years, the FBI and other government agencies have investigated Amdocs more than once. The firm has repeatedly and adamantly denied any security breaches or wrongdoing. But sources tell Fox News that in 1999, the super secret National Security Agency, headquartered in northern Maryland, issued what's called a Top Secret Sensitive Compartmentalized Information report, TS/SCI, warning that records of calls in the United States were getting into foreign hands in Israel, in particular.

Investigators don't believe calls are being listened to, but the data about who is calling whom and when is plenty valuable in itself. An internal Amdocs memo to senior company executives suggests just how Amdocs generated call records could be used. "Widespread data mining techniques and algorithms.... combining both the properties of the customer (e.g., credit rating) and properties of the specific 'behavior....'" Specific behavior, such as who the customers are calling.

The Amdocs memo says the system should be used to prevent phone fraud. But U.S. counterintelligence analysts say it could also be used to spy through the phone system. Fox News has learned that the N.S.A has held numerous classified conferences to warn the F.B.I. and C.I.A. how Amdocs records could be used. At one NSA briefing, a diagram by the Argon national lab was used to show that if the phone records are not secure, major security breaches are possible.

Another briefing document said, "It has become increasingly apparent that systems and networks are vulnerable... Such crimes always involve unauthorized persons, or persons who exceed their authorization...citing on exploitable vulnerabilities."

Those vulnerabilities are growing, because according to another briefing, the U.S. relies too much on foreign companies like Amdocs for high-tech equipment and software. "Many factors have led to increased dependence on code developed overseas.... We buy rather than train or develop solutions'"

U.S. intelligence does not believe the Israeli government is involved in a misuse of information, and Amdocs insists that its data is secure. What U.S. government officials are worried about, however, is the possibility that Amdocs data could get into the wrong hands, particularly organized crime. And that would not be the first thing that such a thing has happened. Fox News has documents of a 1997 drug trafficking case in Los Angeles, in which telephone information, the type that Amdocs collects, was used to "completely compromise the communications of the FBI, the Secret Service, the DEO and the LAPD."

We'll have that and a lot more in the days ahead- Brit.

HUME: Carl, I want to take you back to your report last night on those 60 Israelis who were detained in the antiterror investigation, and the suspicion that some investigators have that they may have picked up information on the 9/11 attacks ahead of time and not passed it on.

There was a report, you'll recall, that the Mossad, the Israeli intelligence agency, did indeed send representatives to the U.S. to warn, just before 9/11, that a major terrorist attack was imminent. How does that leave room for the lack of a warning?

CAMERON: I remember the report, Brit. We did it first internationally right here on your show on the l4th. What investigators are saying is that that warning from the Mossad was nonspecific and general, and they believe that it may have had something to do with the desire to protect what are called sources and methods in the intelligence community. The suspicion being, perhaps those sources and methods were taking place right here in the United States.

The question came up in select intelligence committee on Capitol Hill today. They intend to look into what we reported last night, and specifically that possibility- Brit.

HUME: So in other words, the problem wasn't lack of a warning, the problem was lack of useful details?

CAMERON: Quantity of information.

HUME: All right, Carl, thank you very much."

Here is a copy of the third installment of the *Fox News* reports as posted on the *Free Republic* website- FreeRepublic.com:

Carl Cameron Investigates Part 3 : Comverse, CALEA, Israel and the terror investigation

FreeRepublic.com *"A Conservative News Forum"*

[Threads | Comments | Self-Search | Search | Topics / Post | Bookmark | Abuse | Settings | Help!]

Disclaimer: Opinions posted on Free Republic are those of the individual posters and do not necessarily represent the opinion of Free Republic or its management. All materials posted herein are protected by copyright law and the exemption for fair use of copyrighted works.

Carl Cameron Investigates Part 3 : Comverse, CALEA, Israel and the terror investigation

Crime/Corruption
Source: Fox News: Special Report with Brit Hume
Published: **Dec. 13** Author: **CARL CAMERON**
Posted on **12/14/01 9:22 AM Pacific** by **Plummz**

HUME: Last time we reported on an Israeli-based company called Amdocs Ltd. that generates the computerized records and billing data for nearly every phone call made in America. As Carl Cameron reported, U.S. investigators digging into the 9/11 terrorist attacks fear that suspects may have been tipped off to what they were doing by information leaking out of Amdocs.

In tonight's report, we learn that the concern about phone security extends to another company, founded in Israel, that provides the technology that the U.S. government uses for electronic eavesdropping. Here is Carl Cameron's third report.

(BEGIN VIDEOTAPE)

CARL CAMERON, FOX NEWS CORRESPONDENT (voice-over): The company is Comverse Infosys, a subsidiary of an Israeli-run private telecommunications firm, with offices throughout the U.S. It provides wiretapping equipment for law enforcement. Here's how wiretapping works in the U.S.

Every time you make a call, it passes through the nation's elaborate network of switchers and routers run by the phone companies. Custom computers and software, made by companies like Comverse, are tied into that network to intercept, record and store the wiretapped calls, and at the same time transmit them to investigators.

The manufacturers have continuing access to the computers so they can service them and keep them free of glitches. This process was authorized by the 1994 Communications Assistance for Law Enforcement Act, or CALEA. Senior government officials have now told Fox News that while CALEA made wiretapping easier, it has led to a system that is seriously vulnerable to compromise, and may have undermined the whole wiretapping system.

Indeed, Fox News has learned that Attorney General John Ashcroft and FBI Director Robert Mueller were both warned Oct. 18 in a hand-delivered letter from 15 local, state and federal law enforcement officials, who complained that "law enforcement's current electronic surveillance capabilities are less effective today than they were at the time CALEA was enacted."

Congress insists the equipment it installs is secure. But the complaint about this system is that the wiretap computer programs made by Comverse have, in effect, a back door through which wiretaps themselves can be intercepted by unauthorized parties.

Adding to the suspicions is the fact that in Israel, Comverse works closely with the Israeli government, and under special programs, gets reimbursed for up to 50 percent of its research and development costs by the Israeli Ministry of Industry and Trade. But investigators within the DEA, INS and FBI have all told Fox News that to pursue or even suggest Israeli spying through Comverse is considered career suicide.

And sources say that while various F.B.I. inquiries into Comverse have been conducted over the years, they've been halted before the actual equipment has ever been thoroughly tested for leaks. A 1999 F.C.C. document indicates several government agencies expressed deep concerns that too many unauthorized non-law enforcement personnel can access the wiretap system. And the FBI's own nondescript office in Chantilly, Virginia that actually oversees the CALEA wiretapping program, is among the most agitated about the threat.

But there is a bitter turf war internally at F.B.I. It is the FBI's office in Quantico, Virginia, that has jurisdiction over awarding contracts and buying intercept equipment. And for years, they've thrown much of the business to Comverse. A

http://www.freerepublic.com/focus/fr/590668/posts   12/30/01

> handful of former U.S. law enforcement officials involved in awarding Comverse government contracts over the years now work for the company.
>
> Numerous sources say some of those individuals were asked to leave government service under what knowledgeable sources call "troublesome circumstances" that remain under administrative review within the Justice Department.
>
> (END VIDEOTAPE)
>
> And what troubles investigators most, particularly in New York, in the counter terrorism investigation of the World Trade Center attack, is that on a number of cases, suspects that they had sought to wiretap and survey immediately changed their telecommunications processes. They started acting much differently as soon as those supposedly secret wiretaps went into place – Brit.
>
> HUME: Carl, is there any reason to suspect in this instance that the Israeli government is involved?
>
> CAMERON: No, there's not. But there are growing instincts in an awful lot of law enforcement officials in a variety of agencies who suspect that it had begun compiling evidence, and a highly classified investigation into that possibility –Brit.
>
> HUME: All right, Carl. Thanks very much.

(Messages from members of Free Republic listed at the end of this post have been removed.)

"Carl Cameron Investigates Part 3: Comverse, CALEA, Israel and the terror investigation

Crime/Corruption
Source: Fox News Special Report with Brit Hume
Published: Dec. 13 Author: CARL CAMERON
Posted on 12/14/01 9:22 AM Pacific by Plummz

HUME: Last time we reported on an Israeli-based company called Amdocs Ltd. that generates the computerized records and billing data for nearly every phone call made in America. As Carl Cameron reported, U.S. investigators digging into the 9/11 terrorist attacks fear that suspects may have been tipped off to what they were doing by information leaking out of Amdocs.

In tonight's report, we learn that the concern about phone security extends to another company, founded in Israel, that provides the technology that the U.S. government uses for electronic eavesdropping. Here is Carl Cameron's third report.

(BEGIN VIDEOTAPE)

CARL CAMERON, FOX NEWS CORRESPONDENT (voice-over): The company is Comverse Infosys, a subsidiary of an Israeli-run private telecommunications firm, with offices throughout the U.S. It provides wiretapping equipment for law enforcement. Here's how wiretapping works in the U.S.

Every time you make a call, it passes through the nation's elaborate network of switchers and routers run by the phone companies. Custom computers and software, made by companies like Comverse, are tied into that network to intercept, record and store the wiretapped calls, and at the same time transmit them to investigators.

The manufacturers have continuing access to the computers so they can service them and keep them free of glitches. This process was authorized by the 1994 Communications Assistance for Law Enforcement Act, or CALEA. Senior government officials have now told Fox News that while CALEA made wiretapping easier, it has led to a system that is seriously vulnerable to compromise, and may have undermined the whole wiretapping system.

Indeed, Fox News has learned that Attorney General John Ashcroft and FBI Director Robert Mueller were both warned Oct. l8 in a hand-delivered letter from 1 5 local, state and federal law enforcement officials, who complained that "law enforcement's current electronic surveillance capabilities are less effective today than they were at the time CALEA was enacted."

Congress insists the equipment it installs is secure. But the complaint about this system is that the wiretap computer programs made by Comverse have, in effect, a back door through which wiretaps themselves can be intercepted by unauthorized parties.

Adding to the suspicions is the fact that in Israel, Comverse works closely with the Israeli government, and under special programs, gets reimbursed for up to 50 percent of its research and development costs by the Israeli Ministry of Industry and Trade. But investigators within the DEA, INS and FBI have all told Fox News that to pursue or even suggest Israeli spying through Comverse is considered career suicide.

And sources say that while various F.B.I. inquiries into Comverse have been conducted over the years, they've been halted before the actual equipment has ever been thoroughly tested for leaks. A 1999 F.C,C. document indicates several government agencies expressed deep concerns that too many unauthorized non-law enforcement personnel can access the wiretap system. And the FBI's own nondescript office in Chantilly, Virginia that actually oversees the CALEA wiretapping program, is among the most agitated about the threat.

But there is a bitter turf war internally at F.B.L It is the FBI's office in Quantico, Virginia, that has jurisdiction over awarding contracts and buying intercept equipment. And for years, they've thrown much of the business to Comverse. A handful of former U.S. law enforcement officials involved in awarding Comverse government contracts over the years now work for the company.

Numerous sources say some of those individuals were asked to leave government service under what knowledgeable sources call "troublesome circumstances" that remain under administrative review within the Justice Department.

(END VIDEOTAPE)

And what troubles investigators most, particularly in New York, in the counter terrorism investigation of the World Trade center attack, is that on a number of cases, suspects that they had sought to wiretap and survey immediately changed their telecommunications processes. They started acting much differently as soon as those supposedly secret wiretaps went into place - Brit.

HUME: Carl, is there any reason to suspect in this instance that the Israeli government is involved?

CAMERON: No, there's not. But there are growing instincts in an awful lot of law enforcement officials in a variety of agencies who suspect that it had begun compiling evidence, and a highly classified investigation into that possibility. - Brit.

HUME: All right, Carl. Thanks very much."

Here is a copy of the fourth and final installment of the *Fox News* reports as posted to the *Free Republic* website-FreeRepublic.com:

FreeRepublic.com *"A Conservative News Forum"*

[Threads | Comments | Self-Search | Search | Topics / Post | Bookmark | Abuse | Settings | Help!]

Disclaimer: Opinions posted on Free Republic are those of the individual posters and do not necessarily represent the opinion of Free Republic or its management. All materials posted herein are protected by copyright law and the exemption for fair use of copyrighted works.

Part 4: Carl Cameron Investigates

Foreign Affairs
Source: FoxNews
Published: **Monday, December 17, 200** Author: **Carl Cameron**
Posted on 12/17/01 5:52 PM Pacific by Phil V.

Part 4: Carl Cameron Investigates

FNC
Carl Cameron
Monday, December 17, 2001

Part 4 of 4

TONY SNOW, HOST: This week, senior correspondent Carl Cameron has reported on a longstanding government espionage investigation. Federal officials this year have arrested or detained nearly 200 Israeli citizens suspected of belonging to an "organized intelligence-gathering operation." The Bush administration has deported most of those arrested after Sept. 11, although some are in custody under the new anti-terrorism law.

Cameron also investigates the possibility that an Israeli firm generated billing data that could be used for intelligence purpose, and describes concerns that the federal government's own wiretapping system may be vulnerable. Tonight, in part four of the series, we'll learn about the probable roots of the probe: a drug case that went bad four years ago in L.A.

(BEGIN VIDEOTAPE)

CARL CAMERON, FOX NEWS CORRESPONDENT (voice-over): Los Angeles, 1997, a major local, state and federal drug investigating sours. The suspects: Israeli organized crime with operations in New York, Miami, Las Vegas, Canada, Israel and Egypt. The allegations: cocaine and ecstasy trafficking, and sophisticated white-collar credit card and computer fraud.

The problem: according to classified law enforcement documents obtained by Fox News, the bad guys had the cops' beepers, cell phones, even home phones under surveillance. Some who did get caught admitted to having hundreds of numbers and using them to avoid arrest.

"This compromised law enforcement communications between LAPD detectives and other assigned law enforcement officers working various aspects of the case. The organization discovered communications between organized crime intelligence division detectives, the FBI and the Secret Service."

Shock spread from the DEA to the FBI in Washington, and then the CIA. An investigation of the problem, according to law enforcement documents, concluded, "The organization has apparent extensive access to database systems to identify pertinent personal and biographical information."

When investigators tried to find out where the information might have come from, they looked at Amdocs, a publicly traded firm based in Israel. Amdocs generates billing data for virtually every call in America, and they do credit checks. The company denies any leaks, but investigators still fear that the firm's data is getting into the wrong hands.

When investigators checked their own wiretapping system for leaks, they grew concerned about potential vulnerabilities in the computers that intercept, record and store the wiretapped calls. A main contractor is Comverse Infosys, which works closely with the Israeli government, and under a special grant program, is reimbursed for up to 50 percent of its research and development costs by Israel's Ministry of Industry and Trade.

Asked this week about another sprawling investigation and the detention of 60 Israelis since Sept. 11, the Bush administration treated the questions like hot potatoes.

ARI FLEISCHER, WHITE HOUSE PRESS SECRETARY: I would just refer you to the Department of Justice with that. I'm not familiar with the report.

COLIN POWELL, SECRETARY OF STATE: I'm aware that some Israeli citizens have been detained. With respect to why they're being detained and the other aspects of your question – whether it's because they're in intelligence services, or what they were doing – I will defer to the Department of Justice and the FBI to answer that.

(END VIDEOTAPE)

CAMERON: Beyond the 60 apprehended or detained, and many deported since Sept. 11, another group of 140 Israeli individuals have been arrested and detained in this year in what government documents describe as "an organized intelligence gathering operation," designed to "penetrate government facilities." Most of those individuals said they had served in the Israeli military, which is compulsory there.

But they also had, most of them, intelligence expertise, and either worked for Amdocs or other companies in Israel that specialize in wiretapping. Earlier this week, the Israeli embassy in Washington denied any spying against or in the United States – Tony.

SNOW: Carl, we've heard the comments from Ari Fleischer and Colin Powell. What are officials saying behind the scenes?

CAMERON: Well, there's real pandemonium described at the FBI, the DEA and the INS. A lot of these problems have been well known to some investigators, many of who have contributed to the reporting on this story. And what they say is happening is supervisors and management are now going back and collecting much of the information, because there's tremendous pressure from the top levels of all of those agencies to find out exactly what's going on.

At the DEA and the FBI already a variety of administration reviews are

> under way, in addition to the investigation of the phenomenon. They want to find out how it is all this has come out, as well as be very careful because of the explosive nature and very political ramifications of the story itself – Tony.
>
> SNOW: All right, Carl, thanks.
>
> Part I
>
> Part II
>
> Part III

(Messages from members of Free Republic listed at the end of this post have been removed.)

"Part 4: Carl Cameron Investigates

Foreign Affairs
Source: FoxNews
Published: Monday, December 17, 200 Author: Carl Cameron
Posted on l2/ll/0l 5:52 PM Pacific by Phil V.
Part 4: Carl Cameron Investigates

Part 4 of4

TONY SNOW, HOST: This week, senior correspondent Carl Cameron has reported on a longstanding government espionage investigation. Federal officials this year have arrested or detained nearly 200 Israeli citizens suspected of belonging to an "organized intelligence gathering operation." The Bush administration has deported most of those arrested after Sept. 11, although some are in custody under the new antiterrorism law.

Cameron also investigates the possibility that an Israeli firm generated billing data that could be used for intelligence purpose, and describes concerns that the federal government's own wiretapping system may be vulnerable.

Tonight, in part four of the series, we learn about the probable roots of the probe: a drug case that went bad four years ago in L.A.

(BEGIN VIDEOTAPE)

CARL CAMERON, FOX NEWS CORRESPONDENT (voice-over): Los Angeles, 1997, a major local, state and federal drug investigating sours. The suspects: Israeli organized crime with operations in New York, Miami, Las Vegas, Canada, Israel and Egypt. The allegations: cocaine and ecstasy trafficking and sophisticated white collar credit card and computer fraud.

The problem: according to classified law enforcement documents obtained by Fox News, the bad guys had the cops' beepers, cell phones, even home phones under surveillance. Some who did get caught admitted to having hundreds of numbers and using them to avoid arrest.

"This compromised law enforcement communications between LAPD detectives and other assigned law enforcement officers working various aspects of the case. The organization discovered communications between organized crime intelligence division detectives, the FBI and the Secret Service."

Shock spread from the DEA to the FBI in Washington, and then the CIA. An investigation of the problem, according to law enforcement documents, concluded, "The organization has apparent extensive access to database systems to identify pertinent personal and biographical information."

When investigators tried to find out where the information might have come from, they looked at Amdocs, a publicly traded firm based in Israel. Amdocs generates billing data for virtually every call in America, and they do credit checks. The company denies any leaks, but investigators still fear that the firm's data is getting into the wrong hands.

When investigators checked their own wiretapping system for leaks, they grew concerned about potential vulnerabilities in the computers that intercept, record and store the wiretapped calls. A main contractor is Comverse Infosys, which works closely with the Israeli government, and under a special grant program, is reimbursed for up to 50-percent of its research and development costs by Israel's Ministry of Industry and Trade.

Asked this week about another sprawling investigation and the detention of 60 Israeli since Sept. 11, the Bush administration treated the questions like hot potatoes.

ARI FLEISCHER, WHITE HOUSE PRESS SECRETARY: I would just refer you to the Department of Justice with that. I'm not familiar with the report.

COLIN POWELL, SECRETARY OF STATE: I'm aware that some Israeli citizens have been detained. With respect to why they're being detained and the other aspects of your question- whether it's because they're in intelligence services, or what they were doing- I will defer to the Department of Justice and the FBI to answer that.

(END VIDEOTAPE)

CAMERON: Beyond the 60 apprehended or detained, and many deported since Sept. 11, another group of 140 Israeli individuals have been arrested and detained in this year in what government documents describe as "an organized intelligence gathering operation," designed to penetrate government facilities." Most of those individuals said they had served in the Israeli military, which is compulsory there.

But they also had, most of them, intelligence expertise, and either worked for Amdocs or other companies in Israel that specialize in wiretapping. Earlier this week, the Israeli embassy in Washington denied any spying against or in the United States - Tony.

SNOW: Carl, we've heard the comments from Ari Fleischer and Colin Powell. What are officials saying behind the scenes?

CAMERON: Well, there's real pandemonium described at the FBI, the DEA and the INS. A lot of these problems have been well known to some investigators, many of who have contributed to the reporting on this story. And what they say is happening is supervisors and management are now going back and collecting much of the information, because there's tremendous pressure from the top levers of all of those agencies to find out exactly what's going on.

At the DEA and the FBI already a variety of administration reviews are under way, in addition to the investigation of the phenomenon. They want to find out how it is all this has come out, as well as be very careful because of the explosive nature and very political ramifications of the story itself- Tony.

SNOW: All right, Carl, thanks."

Chapter 4. Targeted for Criminal Prosecution!

As you can tell from the contents of the foregoing chapter, I was very active subsequent to 9/11 in widely disseminating my belief that Zionists in Israel and within our own government had orchestrated the September 11, 2001 terrorist attacks and falsely blamed them on their enemies in the Middle East (Muslims and Arabs). Between December 28, 2001 and December 30, 2001, I was particularly active in widely disseminating a lot of damaging information about Israeli spying against the United States and them using that information to compromise ongoing operations of United States law enforcement.

Only a few days later (on January 9, 2002), fifteen to 20 armed I.R.S. Special Agents were at my home/office in Auburn, New Hampshire with a search warrant and a letter from the U.S. Attorney for the District of New Hampshire informing me that I was the target of a federal criminal investigation into violations of the internal revenue laws!

The I.R.S. Special Agents spent all day at my home/office searching for evidence that I had committed a crime. (They were there from approximately 10:00 a.m. to 8:00 p.m.). They concluded their search by confiscating twenty-three (23) boxes of records from me! However, some of those boxes were simply real estate transaction records left over from when I was a self-employed real estate broker. Other records were of my income tax activities. (Since I did not believe that I was doing anything illegal, I kept meticulous records of my activities.)

I had been conducting income tax seminars for almost five years disseminating Irwin Schiff's information that anyone could legally stop paying federal income taxes. I had also been doing many other things to try to disseminate Schiff's information to as many people as I could.

At the end of each seminar, I informed the attendees that they could either purchase Schiff's books and the audiotape updates to them and learn how to prepare and file

Schiff's Zero Income Tax Returns themselves or they could hire me to prepare for them a Zero Income Tax Return with the latest attachment. The attachment explained the legal and constitutional arguments as to why we did not believe that we owed the tax. I only charged $100.00 to prepare the return, so most people hired me to prepare it for them.

In addition to Schiff's arguments, I had also devised another argument as to why I believed that the federal income tax was illegal. I added it to the tax return attachments that I submitted with my own tax returns and that I prepared for others. It was based on information that I had received from Schiff and then investigated further on my own.

It was because there is a tremendous amount of evidence that after an earlier federal income tax had been deemed unconstitutional by the Supreme Court of the United States in 1895, the current income tax which was instituted in 1916 was only supposed to be levied upon the incomes of wealthy individuals and businesses. And for many years, it was only levied upon those entities. However, over time, Congress gradually and incrementally expanded the scope of the income tax to include the incomes of virtually all individuals and businesses. I believed that that gradual expansion was unconstitutional because it violated the original intent of the Sixteenth Amendment, the Constitutional amendment that allowed for a federal income tax.

I also organized a petition drive regarding my belief that the federal income tax was unconstitutional because it had been expanded beyond the scope of its original intent. It was a petition drive directed to Congress asking them to investigate my evidence and then rectify the situation.

Irwin Schiff had always admonished his followers to not simply take his word for everything that he espoused, but to learn how to do our own legal research and decide for ourselves whether or not we believed that he was correct. He also encouraged us to learn how to defend ourselves civilly in court in case that the I.R.S. ever seized any of our property and how to prosecute a civil lawsuit against the I.R.S. in case we ever felt the need. He also encouraged us to learn how to defend ourselves criminally in court in case the Justice Department ever decided to prosecute us. However, the chances of that happening were unlikely. In the approximately ten years that Schiff and his followers had been filing Zero Income Tax Returns with the I.R.S., no one had been prosecuted.

Even though the I.R.S. had raided my home/office and the U.S. Attorney had informed me that I was the target of a federal criminal investigation, I continued my income tax activities because I was sure that I was not doing anything illegal. I continued to assist my clients and I continued to sell videotapes of my seminar. The assistance to my clients included preparing responses to I.R.S. notices that some of them were receiving.

I Got an Attorney to Represent Me

There was a legal expert living in New Hampshire at the time that all of this was going on who was quite well known. He was not a lawyer, but many lawyers hired him to prepare legal briefs for them. He had also represented some well-known New Hampshire individuals in court in civil cases. His name was Theo Kamisinski.

I ran into Theo at some point and told him about being raided by the I.R.S. and being informed by the U.S. Attorney that I was the target of a federal criminal investigation. He informed me that because I had very little savings or income and because I was a target of a federal criminal investigation, I was entitled to a court-appointed attorney. He recommended that I apply to the U.S. District Court for one and that I ask for an attorney from the local Federal Defender's Office named Jonathan Saxe to represent me. (A Federal Defender is the same thing as a Public Defender, except on the federal court level.) So I applied for Attorney Saxe to represent me and my application was granted.

I met with Attorney Saxe at his office in Concord, New Hampshire shortly thereafter. The first thing that he asked me to explain was why I believed the federal income tax was voluntary and why I believed that no one was required to pay it. So I informed him of Irwin Schiff's major arguments. After we discussed them for a while, he informed me that it was his belief that most of Schiff's arguments were incorrect and that I should not be using them, nor advising others to use them.

I already had to discontinue using some of Schiff's arguments in battles with the I.R.S. prior to being targeted for prosecution by the Justice Department because I knew that they would not hold up in an actual court. It was one thing to make legal arguments about federal income taxes on attachments to Zero Income Tax Returns or in Collection Due Process Hearings with I.R.S. agents, but it was another thing to make some arguments in the appeal of CDP Hearing determinations in U.S. District Court. Over the years, federal courts had rejected some of the legal arguments made by tax protestors. Anyone raising those arguments in subsequent legal proceedings were subject to having court sanctions imposed on them. That could include having a fine levied against them. So I had to discontinue using in federal court any of Schiff's arguments that the courts has already rejected.

Attorney Saxe informed me that he rarely met with a potential client before he or she was indicted. He advised me to authorize him to contact the Assistant U.S. Attorney assigned to my case, William E. Morse, and ask about a plea deal for me. (A plea deal is a recommendation by the prosecutor to the judge in a criminal case for a lighter sentence if that person were to plead "guilty" to committing a certain crime or crimes.)

I was not really interested in taking a plea agreement because I did not believe that I had committed any crimes. However, I was interested in what the Government would offer, so I authorized Attorney Saxe to contact Attorney Morse.

Attorney Morse responded to Attorney Saxe a few weeks later. He said that the Government would be willing to recommend to the judge in my case that, in the event that I did get indicted, I only receive a two (2) year prison sentence for pleading "guilty" to committing some unspecified crime. Since I was not interested in pleading "guilty" to a crime that I did not believe I had committed, I informed Attorney Saxe of that and told him to decline Attorney Morse's offer.

In my discussion with Attorney Saxe, he informed me that if I were to be indicted by the Government on criminal charges, he would not be able to use any of Irwin Schiff's income tax arguments as a basis for my defense. So I thanked him for his services and told him that I would no longer need them. If the Government were to indict me, I would defend myself.

I Tried to Enlighten My Grand Jury

The letter that I received on January 9, 2002 informing me that I was the target of a federal criminal investigation also informed me that a federal grand jury would be conducting the investigation and would decide if I should be indicted. I was informed that if I wished to testify before the grand jury prior to it making a decision, I could do so by contacting Assistant U.S. Attorney Morse. I was interested in explaining to the grand jury that I had not done anything illegal, so I contacted Attorney Morse. He informed me that he would notify me of when I would be able to meet with them.

From the legal research I had conducted via material from the Erwin Rommel School of Law, I learned that modern grand juries had long ago abandoned their true investigative duties and had simply become "rubber stamps" for whatever the prosecutors desired. I was interested in trying to inform the grand jury investigating me that it had a right to investigate my case on its own without being controlled by the prosecutors.

In earlier times, grand juries were very powerful. They would conduct their own investigations into whether or not crimes had been committed and whether or not to indict someone. Prosecutors were not even allowed to be present during grand jury proceedings! Then around 1906, a U.S. legislator decided that allowing prosecutors into grand jury proceedings would be a good idea and he got legislation to that effect enacted.

It did not take long for prosecutors to take over the whole grand jury process and grand juries simply became a rubber stamps for the prosecutors. In fact, since grand juries were no longer conducting their own private investigations into matters, a new government agency had to be formed. It was established in 1908 and was named the Federal Bureau of Investigations. Since I knew that the grand jury investigating me had the power to investigate my case on its own without being controlled by the prosecutors, I wanted to inform it of that fact. (Grand juries that expel the prosecutors and investigate matters on their own are called "Runaway Grand Juries." That was what I wanted.)

I was finally contacted by Assistant U.S. Attorney Morse and told that I could appear before the grand jury on Wednesday, March 5, 2003. Attorney Morse also informed me that the only way that I would be allowed to testify was if I agreed to be questioned (examined) by him and/or another professional prosecutor. I would not be allowed to present any testimony on my own. I was hesitant to do so because I knew that a professional prosecutor could twist my words and make it seem as though I was stating something that I was not really stating. However, since I really wanted an opportunity to inform the grand jury about its true power and that I had not committed any illegal acts, I agreed to do so.

When I got to the grand jury area at the federal courthouse in Concord, New Hampshire, I was taken aside by a different Assistant U.S. Attorney. This one was specially brought in for my case from the Tax Division of the U.S. Department of Justice in Washington, DC. His name was James W. Chapman. Attorney Chapman reiterated to me that the only way that I would be allowed to testify was if I agreed to be examined by Attorney Morse and/or by him. Again, I agreed.

When the grand jury was ready to accept my testimony, I was taken to the witness stand. Attorney Morse attempted to swear me in, but before he could do so, I began addressing the grand jury members directly and informing them of their power to conduct an unbiased investigation of me on their own. I also informed them that they had the power to even expel the professional prosecutors from the room while they did so!

Attorney Morse tried to get me to stop, but I kept addressing the grand jury. He did not know what to do to get me to stop! I was exposing the whole charade of how the Government had unfairly usurped the power of federal grand juries and the whole grand jury investigative process to an actual federal grand jury! Morse finally ran into the hallway and got a bailiff to try to control me. The prosecutors and I eventually agreed to allow the grand jury to vote on whether or not to allow me to present my testimony on my own or whether I must be examined by the prosecutors. Since the grand jury members had probably been instructed by the prosecutors how to proceed in other proceedings before they got to mine, it was not surprising that they voted to require me to be examined by the prosecutors in order for me to be able to testify before them.

I was led back into the grand jury room and taken to the witness stand. Again Attorney Morse attempted to swear me in. First he asked me if I was willing to allow him and Attorney Chapman to examine me. I told him that I would have to be pretty stupid to agree to allow professional federal prosecutors the opportunity to misconstrue my testimony and attempt to get me to state things on the record that I did not really mean. Attorney Morse then dismissed me from the stand and I left.

I Got Indicted, Arrested, and Arraigned!

Two days later, on March 7, 2003 at around 11:00 am, I went to the Auburn, New Hampshire Post Office to pick up my mail. As I was walking up the walkway to the Post Office, I noticed a black Pontiac Trans Am driving toward the Post Office on its long driveway really slowly. I thought that that was rather odd because most people drive in purposefully, but I really did not think too much about it.

While in the box lobby retrieving my mail, I was approached by a number of armed I.R.S. Special Agents in SWAT Team fashion and arrested! Some of them had been in the Trans Am. Fortunately, they arrested me peacefully! They informed me that the federal grand jury that I had appeared before just two days earlier had indicted me (at the behest of the U.S. Attorney) on eighteen (18) felony violations of the internal revenue laws! (Whenever the

Justice Department indicts someone, it brings as many charges as it can in order to attempt to coerce that defendant into pleading "guilty" to a lesser charge. That is called "stacking charges." If a person pleads "guilty" to some charge or charges rather than forcing the Government to take them to trial, the prosecutors and the judges will not have to do as much work.)

Seventeen of the 18 counts brought against me were for violations of 26 U.S. Code § 7206-- "preparing and filing for myself and for others federal income tax returns which I knew and believed to be false." (Two counts of filing them for myself and fifteen counts of preparing them for others.) The eighteenth charge was for violating 26 U.S. Code § 7212(a])--"Obstructing and impeding the administration of the tax laws."

All of the charges against me hinged on the fact that I knew and believed the tax returns that I had prepared and filed for myself and for others to be false. However, I did not believe that they were false! Moreover, I had spent almost the past five (5) years doing everything that I could think of to try to convince others of what I believed!

The I.R.S. Special Agents then transported me to the U.S. Marshal's Office at the federal courthouse in Concord, New Hampshire to await arraignment. (Usually when a tax protestor or other white-collar defendant is about to be indicted, he or she is allowed to simply appear at the courthouse on their own to be arraigned. Apparently Assistant U.S. Attorney Morse was so upset by my attempt to inform the grand jury of its rightful power that he had me arrested instead!)

While I was waiting to be arraigned by a U.S. magistrate judge, I was approached by a slender, shaggy-haired, bearded attorney who informed me that he had been appointed by the magistrate judge to represent me. His name was Michael Shklar. I told him that I did not need nor want to be represented by him because I was going to represent myself. He told me to wait and we would see what the magistrate judge had to say about the issue.

Federal Criminal Defense Is a Racket!

The reason that I did not want to be represented by an attorney was because I had learned from my studies at the Erwin Rommel School of Law that criminal defense attorneys do not really represent their clients as well as they should. They make their clients think that they are going to represent them optimally, but in reality, they only provide an adequate defense up to a certain point and then they stop. That is because the criminal justice system in the United States is a racket!

The judges (many of whom were former federal prosecutors themselves) do whatever they have to do in order to to ensure that the Government prosecutors prevail in their prosecutions. Defense attorneys who want to participate in this lucrative racket realize that they have to cooperate with the judges and the prosecutors in order to be allowed to. Defense attorneys who do not cooperate are ostracized by the judges.

One of the ways that that is accomplished is by the judges refusing to appoint them to represent indigent clients (as court-appointed attorneys). Another way is for the judges to rule against most of the actions of the defense attorneys. So defense attorneys know that if they "play ball" with the judges and the prosecutors and only defend their clients up to a certain point, they will get a lot more defense work. (I cannot tell you how many times my fellow inmates told me when I was incarcerated with them that their attorneys hardly did anything to represent them. The attorneys had convinced the inmates that they were going to do really good jobs for them, but when it came time to do so, they never did. Before they knew it, they had been convicted and incarcerated! And many of those attorneys had collected huge amounts of money from the inmates!)

I was finally taken to a courtroom to be arraigned by a magistrate judge. His name was James Muirhead. Before he arraigned me, he informed me that Attorney Shklar was there to act as my court-appointed attorney if I wished to have one. He told me that Attorney Shklar was Jewish and that he was a good attorney. He went on to praise Attorney Shklar's mother who, if I remember correctly, was an educator and an author. I think that she had been an educator in Boston and that she had written about the Holocaust. I thought that it was rather odd for Magistrate Judge Muirhead to be telling me all of this, but I did not say anything about it. (I later learned that Attorney Shklar smoked cigarettes, lived in a very rural area of New Hampshire, and I think that he drove a Volkswagen Beetle. He was probably a former "Hippie."I doubt if he had ever even defended anyone charged criminally in a federal court before.)

I informed Magistrate Judge Muirhead that I did not want to be represented by an attorney; rather, I wished to represent myself. He told me that I could do that, but that he was also going to appoint Attorney Shklar to be my Standby Counsel in case I changed my mind. I agreed to that arrangement.

Magistrate Judge Muirhead asked me how I pleaded to each of the eighteen (18) felony counts the Government was charging me with. Since I did not believe that I was guilty of committing any of the charges, I pleaded "Not Guilty" to each one of them. Magistrate Judge Muirhead then told me that a date would be set for my trial and he asked me if I intended to appear for it. I told him that I did. He then released me on $100,000 Personal Recognizance bail. (That meant that I did not have to pledge any money in order to be released.) I believe that I was then ordered not to leave the state without the permission of the U.S. Attorney. The Docket Number of my case is 03-CR-036-PB. ("PB" are the initials of the judge assigned to my case-Chief Judge Paul Barbadoro.)

Preparing My Defense

So I had learned how to challenge the I.R.S. in its imposition of federal income taxes using federal tax law. And I had learned how to conduct lawsuits against I.R.S. agents, protect myself and my clients from civil actions from the Government, and appeal adverse I.R.S. Collection Due Process determinations using federal civil law. Now I found myself in the position of having to learn how to defend myself from criminal charges using federal criminal law.

Learning to use the law is not that difficult once one learns how to navigate through it. There are two major types of law—civil law and criminal law. And each type has its own set of rules that one must follow. For federal civil law, it is the Federal Rules of Civil Procedure. For federal criminal law, it is the Federal Rules of Criminal Procedure. First you have to learn the rules. (Citizens have to follow the rules. The Government has more leeway because the judge is also a Government employee will allow the Government more leniency.)

However, each U.S. District Court also has its own set of rules in addition to those just mentioned. So you have to learn those rules as well. Then you have to learn the indexing system of the decisions of previously decided cases so that you can those decisions to apply to your case. Once you can do that, you are ready to proceed.

There were a few news reports over the next few days regarding my arrest and arraignment. Each felony count with which I was being charged carried a maximum penalty of up to three (3) years in prison and up to a $250,000 fine! So the news reports stated that I was facing up to fifty-four (54) years in prison and up to a $4,500,000 fine! However, that is not the way that sentencing in federal jurisprudence works. Rather, there is a set of Federal Sentencing Guidelines that judges must use when sentencing an individual, company, or whatever.

One of the things that I learned after being indicted was that an undercover I.R.S. Special Agent had attended one of my income tax seminars a few months earlier. After that seminar, he made an appointment to come to my home/office to discuss me preparing a couple of Zero Income Tax Returns for him-one for the current year and one for the previous year. I subsequently prepared them both for him.

A few days later, I received a notice from the court informing me that a Final Pre-Trial Conference between the prosecutors and myself was scheduled for April 21, 2003. My trial was scheduled to commence on May 6th and last possibly two weeks.

Discovery

One of the things that has to be done before going to trial is a procedure called Discovery. This is where each party discloses to the other party all of the evidence it has and intends to submit into evidence at trial. I contacted Attorney Morse and asked him when I could examine the Government's evidence against me. He told me that he would let me know. He also told me that the evidence that seized from my home/office was at an I.R.S. office in Portsmouth, New Hampshire, 45 miles away from my home. The Government's own evidence against me was at Attorney Morse's office.

Since it was obvious to me that I was going to need more time to prepare to defend myself against the Government, I filed a motion with the court for a continuance. Judge Barbadoro granted my motion. The Final Pre-Trial Conference was rescheduled to August 25, 2003 and my trial was rescheduled to commence on September 3, 2003.

After I realized that the income tax arguments from Schiff that I had been using and promoting for the past few years were faulty, I decided to no longer use them. I also advised all of my income tax clients that they should not use them either. However, I figured that it was still prudent to continue using the income tax argument that I had devised, *i.e.*, that the federal income tax was unconstitutional because it was illegally expanded beyond its original intent of only taxing the profits of wealthy individuals and businesses. We had already been using it in conjunction with Schiff's arguments, so it was not as if we were beginning anything new. So I advised my income tax clients of that as well. Many of them agreed to continue using it.

In the interim, the Government decided that it needed to amend the original indictment handed down by the grand jury. So the Government got them to approve a superseding indictment. A new arraignment was scheduled for me to plead to the amended charges on April 30, 2003. However, it was essentially the same as the original indictment—18 felony counts against me.

On April 25, 2003, I went to the I.R.S. office in Portsmouth, New Hampshire to begin reviewing the evidence that the I.R.S. agents had confiscated from my home/office. I also asked for copies of many of the pertinent documents. It took me three days to review everything!

On May 15, 2003, I went to the U.S. Attorney's Office in Concord, New Hampshire to begin reviewing the purported evidence that the Government had against me. One of the first things that I saw was a three-ring binder with an 8 ½" x 11" photograph slipped into the cover. The photograph was of a black swan! Clever, huh? Steven Swan—Black Swan!

Motion Practice

One of the things I learned from the Erwin Rommel School of Law was that very few federal criminal defendants ever go to trial. That is because defendants in those trials never get fair trials! The judges will do everything in their power to ensure that the Government prevails. And the prosecutors and their witnesses will lie in order to obtain convictions for the Government! So defendants are coerced into pleading "guilty" by their attorneys, even if they are not guilty! The risk is simply too great!

Because of this fact, if a defendant does go to trial, there is a good possibility that the prosecutors or the judge is going to make a number of major mistakes. They are simply too inexperienced at conducting trials to be effective. And those mistakes can lead to a conviction being overturned on appeal. But a defendant has to go through the whole process and try to get the prosecutors and the judge to make as many mistakes as possible. And you have to document those mistakes, i.e., get them on the record.

The way to get judges and the prosecutors to make as many mistakes as possible is to raise as many issues as possible. One way to do that is through the filing of pre-trial motions asking for relief for one thing or another. Defense attorneys rarely file pre-trial motions on behalf of their clients. That is because, as I disclosed earlier, they are a parties to conspiracies against defendants! I, on the other hand, filed dozens of pre-trial motions in my case.

I filed a number of different motions to dismiss the charges against me for various reasons. Then the prosecutor had to respond to each one of my motions. Then the judge had to rule on each motion. Not surprisingly, virtually all of them were denied by the judge. Then I often filed a Motion for Reconsideration, to which the prosecutor had to respond and on which the judge again had to rule. I think that the judge and the prosecutors played a lot less golf while my case was active! But at least I got those issues on the record and eligible for those denials to be overturned by the appeals court.

Another way to get issues on the record is to raise them at the trial itself via trial motions, objections, etc. And that I intended to do.

As it became clear to me that I would need still more time in which to defend myself against the Government, on July 17, 2003, I filed another motion with the court for a continuance. Judge Barbadoro granted my motion on July 30, 2003. The Final Pre-Trial Conference was rescheduled to October 24, 2003 and my trial was rescheduled to commence on November 4, 2003.

On July 22, 2003, I filed with the court a motion to dismiss the charges against me because the federal income tax was unconstitutional because it had been expanded by Congress beyond the original intent of the Sixteenth Amendment.

One of the reasons that I believed that the information Schiff had been espousing was true was because for many years neither he nor any of his many thousands of followers who filed Zero Income Tax Returns with the I.R.S. had experienced any major negative repercussions from the I.R.S. or from the Justice Department. So I deduced that the Government's failure to do anything to enjoin Schiff from espousing his views or practicing them made the Government complicit in me practicing them. So I filed a motion with the court asking it to dismiss the charges filed against me because the Government was complicit in my course of conduct. Not surprisingly, the judge denied my motion.

I Tried to Warn Schiff's Other Followers

After I came to the realization that Schiff's income tax arguments were no longer viable, I decided that it was my duty to try to warn his many thousands followers of that fact so that they would not be targeted for prosecution by the Justice Department as I had been. I thought that they might be targeted because with the election of President George W. Bush in 2000, his Justice Department and his Internal Revenue Service may be taking a harder line with income tax protestors than the previous President Clinton administration had.

So I contacted Schiff and as many of his followers as I could through discussion groups to which I belonged. I explained to them why I believed that Schiff's arguments were incorrect and why I believed that they should no longer employ them. However, my efforts were not warmly received. Most of these individuals were ardent followers of Schiff and they trusted him more than they trusted me.

I also launched a website in which I explained argument by argument why I believed that Schiff's information was incorrect. It was located at SchiffIsWrong.info.

One of Schiff's primary arguments against the federal income tax being mandatory was that there is no law making anyone "liable" to pay it. His reasoning went like this: There are many different types of federal taxes. And for each federal tax, there is one law that "imposes" the tax and another law which states who shall be "liable" to pay the tax. Except for the income tax, that is. There is a law that imposes the tax. However, there is no law which specifically uses the word "liable" with respect to paying it. So Schiff reasoned that that meant that the tax was not mandatory.

Schiff further believed that the Congress purposely wrote the federal Income Tax Code in such a convoluted and confusing manner as it did in an attempt to hide the fact that there is no law making the federal income tax mandatory. Unfortunately, Schiff did not comprehend how much latitude judges have in interpreting the laws of this country. That is one of the things that I learned from doing a tremendous amount of legal research over the years—first in regard to tax law and civil law and later in regard to criminal law.

There is nothing in the law that states that a federal tax law must use the term "liable" when delineating who is liable to pay a federal tax. And there is a statute in the Internal Revenue Code which states who shall be liable to pay federal income taxes; it just does not use the word "liable" in that statute. Schiff failed to realize that federal judges have a tremendous amount of latitude in determining whether or not a statute makes a person liable to pay federal income taxes.

In another effort to publicize my belief that Schiff's arguments were incorrect, I filed a civil lawsuit against him in federal court in Las Vegas, Nevada. (I was required to file it there because that was where he was located.) Since Schiff was a nationally-known figure, my lawsuit garnered some publicity, but it is difficult to quantify how well it registered with his supporters. I knew that I would not be able to collect any money from Schiff because he routinely informed his followers that they should keep any money they had in foreign banks-out of the potential reach of the I.R.S. I also knew that the I.R.S. had substantial liens against Schiff. Those liens would also have precluded me from collecting any money from him.

Despite all of my efforts, Schiff continued espousing the messages that he had been espousing for years. He continued with his nightly radio program, his business, his seminars, his media interviews, everything. Even though I, one of his most ardent supporters and promoters, had been targeted by the I.R.S. purportedly for espousing his revelations and standing up to the I.R.S. and for assisting others in standing up to the I.R.S., he simply told his followers that I must have not followed his suggestions correctly.

Many people believe that Irwin Schiff was a shill for the Government, i.e., that he propounded his income tax theories in order to purposely get individuals into trouble with the I.R.S. I do not believe that that was true. I think that Schiff truly believed that there was no law making the federal income tax mandatory and that no one was legally required to pay it. He certainly spent a major portion of his life attempting to convince others of that. And he probably died believing it. (He passed away on October 16, 2015.)

Chapter 5. Not Targeted Because of My Income Tax Activities

As time went by after I was indicted by the Government, I was quite surprised that I was the only one of Irwin Schiff's many thousands of followers who was targeted. Schiff himself was not even targeted! And as I continued to hear Schiff on his nightly radio program counseling individuals that anyone could legally stop paying federal income taxes and encouraging them to do so, I was even more surprised. I would have thought that if the Justice Department had wanted to prosecute Schiff followers, it would also have targeted Schiff himself. (Schiff and a couple of his associates were eventually prosecuted a couple of years later, but to wait so long was highly unusual. These actions were not the usual prosecutorial procedures employed by the Justice Department.)

Usually when the Justice Department decides to prosecute someone criminally, they charge as many co-defendants as possible and try to get them to testify against each other in exchange for less severe sentences for themselves. That way the prosecutors and the judges do not have to work as hard as they normally would. They begin with lesser figures to an enterprise and then work their way to the top. However, life went on as usual for Schiff and his many followers. (I think that one of the reasons that Schiff was even prosecuted at all was because I complained so much about me being the only one of his many followers to be prosecuted. It is only human nature for someone to feel legally wronged if they are prosecuted criminally by the Government for doing something and the person whose information he or she was disseminating was allowed to continue disseminating it himself. If I had not complained so much, Schiff may never have been prosecuted at all!)

So I began to think that there might have been another reason why I had been targeted by the Government, especially since I had been disseminating Schiff's information for almost 5 years without any major negative repercussions. Perhaps it was because I had been widely disseminating just before I was raided by the I.R.S. my belief that Zionists in the United States and in Israel had orchestrated the 9/11 terrorist attacks against the United States. It might also have been all of the other derogatory evidence I had been widely disseminating against the Zionists and against Israel just before I was raided.

It has been stated that, to determine who really controls society as a whole, all one has to do is determine who is not allowed to be criticized. In some respects, Jews fall into that category!

Virtually anyone who criticizes anything that a Jew does or says is automatically labeled an "Anti-Semite" and a "Racist!" That just show you how much power and control they really have. And to label anyone who criticizes a Jew a "racist" begs another question. Are those who practice Judaism practicing a religion or are they members of a separate race? They must be members of a separate race, otherwise, their critics would not be labeled "racists."

Some of the extremely powerful Jewish Zionists who I believed were dual loyalists to both the United States and Israel and who were in power when I was raided by the I.R.S. were Director of the C.I.A., George Tenet; F.B.I Director, Louis Freeh, Deputy Secretary of Defense, Paul Wolfowitz; head of the Criminal Division of the U.S. Department of Justice, Michael Chertoff; Deputy Secretary of State, Richard Armitage; 1st Assistant Secretary of Defense for Global Strategic Affairs, Richard Perle; National Security Council operative, Elliott Abrams; White House Press Secretary for President George W. Bush, Ari Fleischer; one of the Pentagon's Defense Policy Board members, Kenneth Adelman; one of President Bush's speechwriters, David Frum; and head of the Defense Department's Office of Special Plans, Douglas Feith. (Michael Chertoff later went on to become the Secretary of Homeland Security under President George W. Bush.)

Powerful Zionist dual loyalists in the media at that time I was raided by the I.R.S. were co-founder of *The Weekly Standard* magazine, William Kristol; *U.S. News and World* Report owner, Mortimer Zuckerman, political commentator and columnist, Charles Krauthammer; veteran *60 Minutes* correspondent Mike Wallace, syndicated columnist Jonah Goldberg; radio talk-show host, Michael Savage; *Wall Street Journal* editor and columnist, Max Boot; and many, many more.

This possibility that I was targeted by the Government for disseminating negative evidence about the Zionists became even more plausible when I discovered that the brother of the head of the Defense Department's Office of Special Plans, Douglas Feith, was the head of the criminal division of the New Hampshire U.S. Attorney's Office, the very office which was prosecuting me! His name is Donald Feith. (Douglas Feith and the Office of Special Plans were also instrumental in the United States' invasion of Iraq based upon flawed information.)

I can imagine that the conversation between Douglas Feith and Donald Feith went something like this:

Douglas Feith: "Donald, there is a guy in New Hampshire who is widely disseminating his beliefs that Zionists orchestrated 9/11 as a False Flag operation in which they blamed the attacks on Muslims and Arabs in order to dupe the United States into greatly expanding its military presence in the Middle East and waging war on the Zionist's enemies. He is also widely disseminating other derogatory information about Zionists. His name is Steven Swan and he lives in Auburn."

Donald Feith: "Let me look into it."

Donald Feith: "Oh yeah. Steven Swan is a tax protestor. It will be easy to silence him. We will prosecute him, convict him, and shut him up. Consider it done."

My Motion to Dismiss Because of Vindictive and/or Selective Prosecution

In September of 2003, I widely distributed to many individuals, news organizations, elected officials, etc. my belief that I was being vindictively and selectively prosecuted because I had widely disseminated my belief that Zionists in the United States and in Israel had orchestrated the 9/11 terrorist attacks and all of the other negative evidence I had been widely disseminating against the Zionists just before I was raided by the I.R.S.

I also wrote letters to U.S. Attorney Colantuono (New Hampshire) and Assistant U.S. Attorney Morse about my belief that I was being vindictively and selectively prosecuted by the Government for disseminating evidence detrimental to Zionists. I asked them not to destroy any evidence that they might have regarding that belief.

I also wrote letters to federal, state, and local officials (including President Bush) and law enforcement personnel about that belief and also my belief that my personal safety might be in jeopardy because I was exposing so much negative information about these ruthless, heinous individuals and groups.

On September 13, 2003, I moved to Manchester, New Hampshire, the largest city in the state. Shortly thereafter, Manchester Police Detective Captain Jim Winn contacted me about the letter I had written to the chief of police about my concern for my safety. He asked me to meet with him to discuss the issue, which I did. At the conclusion of the meeting, he told me to contact the Manchester Police Department immediately if anything suspicious happened.

On October 14, 2003, I filed a motion asking Judge Barbadoro to dismiss the charges against me because I was a victim of unlawful vindictive and/or selective prosecution by the Government in an attempt to prevent me from continuing to widely distribute derogatory information about extremely powerful Zionists subsequent to the September 11, 2001 terrorist attacks against the United States. Here is that motion: (I do not have an actual copy of the motion to insert here, so I am simply including the text of it. Most of the exhibits referred to in the motion have already been reproduced in this book.)

UNITED STATES DISTRICT COURT
FOR THE DISTRICT OF NEW HAMPSHIRE

UNITED STATES OF AMERICA	)
Plaintiff	)
v.	) Criminal No. 03-36-01-B
	)
STEVEN A. SWAN	)
Defendant	)
_____	)

DEFENDANT'S MOTION TO DISMISS SUPERCEDING [SIC] INDICTMENT OR FOR AN EVIDENTIARY HEARING OR DISCOVERY BECAUSE OF VINDICTIVE AND/OR SELECTIVE PROSECUTION BY THE GOVERNMENT

I, Steven A. Swan, the Defendant in this matter, move this Court to dismiss the Superceding [sic] Indictment against me or to order an evidentiary hearing or for the Government to provide me with discovery because I have been vindictively and/or selectively prosecuted by the Government in retaliation for me exercising my right to free speech and expression under the First Amendment to the Constitution of the United States. In support of this motion, I offer the following:

BACKGROUND

1. For many years, I have been an outspoken critic of what I perceive to be corruption by federal government officials and the manipulation of those officials by wealthy and powerful members of special interest groups.

2. The methods which I have employed over the years to disseminate my criticism of those government officials and special interest groups have been through widely-distributed opinion releases using e-mail and faxes; letters-to-the-editor and guest editorials of various newspapers, magazines, and Internet news and opinion sites; calls and faxes to radio and television talk shows; newspaper, magazine, radio, television, and Internet interviews; the income tax seminars I previously conducted; etc.

3. Over the years, I have criticized all kinds of what I perceived to be government corruption and manipulation of government officials by wealthy and powerful special interest groups. However, just prior to January 9, 2002 (when I.R.S. Special Agents executed search warrants at my home and the U.S. Attorney for the District of New Hampshire informed me that I was the target of a criminal investigation), I had been especially outspoken about what I perceived to be the culpability of Israel and some of our country's high-ranking government officials in the September 11, 2001 terrorist attacks against the United States.

4. Some of the high-ranking federal government officials of whom I have been highly critical over the years have been Jews who seem to have a dual loyalty to both the United States and Israel. Some of the members of the present Bush Administration who fit into that category are Central Intelligence Agency (CIA) Director George Tenet, Deputy Secretary of Defense Paul Wolfowitz, Under Secretary of Defense Richard Armitage, Defense Policy Board member and former its chairman Richard Perle, and Special Advisor to the National Security Council, Elliot Abrams. These men have been very instrumental in the Bush Administration's unwavering support for Israel no matter how many atrocities it commits against the Palestinian people and its neighboring countries and they also could have been very instrumental in the planning, execution, and subsequent cover-up of the attacks. These men were also very instrumental in lobbying for the United States invasion of one of Israel's neighbors and enemies, Iraq, earlier this year. At the time of the September 11, 2001 terrorist attacks on the United States, former Federal Bureau of Investigation (FBI) Director Louis Freeh and former White House Spokesman Ari Fleischer also fit into the category of high-ranking Jews in the Bush Administration who seem to be dual-loyalists to both Israel and the United States and who could have been complicit in certain facets of the attacks. I am sure that there are many more people who fit into this category who I am unaware of or who I cannot recollect at this moment.

5. There are also many influential Jewish dual-loyalists to both the United States and Israel in the news media who could have assisted in obfuscating the fact that Israel and others loyal to it contrived the attacks in order to drag the United States into wars with all of Israel's enemies. Some of them are William Kristol, editor of <u>The Weekly Standard</u>, Mortimer Zuckerman, editor and publisher of <u>U.S. News and World Reports</u>, national radio talk show host syndicated columnist Michael Savage, Mike Wallace of CBS Television's <u>60 Minutes</u>, syndicated columnists Charles Krauthammer and Jonah Goldberg, and the list goes on and on. Not to mention the fact that many national radio and television talk show hosts, such as Rush Limbaugh, Don Imus, Bill O'Reilly, and Sean Hannity, earn millions of dollars each year apiece because they promote the pro-Israel point of view. And this is also not to mention the fact that three of the world's six largest media companies are run by dual-loyalists to Israel— Gerald Levin, Chief Executive Officer (CEO) of Time Warner; Michael Eisner, CEO of The Walt Disney Company; and Sumner Redstone (formerly known as Murray Rothstein), the CEO of Viacom.

6. There is a phrase in Latin (*qui bono*?) which translates into "Who benefits?" Whenever a major event happens in the world, I ask myself "Who could have benefited the most from that event?" After the September 11, 2001 terrorist attacks on the United States, I pondered who could have benefited the most from those attacks, which resulted in the widespread vilification of Arabs and Muslims by United States citizens and which will probably drag the United States into wars with all of Israel's enemies. (Afghanistan and Iraq seem to be the first two of Israel's enemies to be invaded and conquered by the United States on behalf of Israel.) The answer to my question was obvious—Israel and its many Jewish supporters in this country (many of whom are high-ranking officials in our own government) benefited the most from the terrorist attacks. And the fact that many Jews who are loyal to Israel control much of the news and entertainment media in this country helps to perpetuate the myth that radical Islamic fundamentalists planned and executed the attacks.

7. As further evidence that Israel and those loyal to that country were responsible for the attacks on the United States, realize that it has been over two years since the attacks occurred and there have been no further terrorist attacks in this country. This is true even though the controlled, mainstream media constantly reminds Americans that most Muslims hate freedom and want to kill or injure Americans; even though there are millions of Muslims living in this country; even though travel in this country is virtually unrestricted; and even though guns and ammunition, gasoline, gunpowder, chemicals, and other explosives are readily available. If Muslims were truly intent on killing or maiming Americans as the mainstream media would have us believe, we would have seen many other terrorist attacks against Americans within our own borders over the past two years. The fact that we have not seen them is evidence that the September 11, 2001 terrorist attacks were contrived. Furthermore, I would not be surprised to see another contrived terrorist attack against the United States prior to the 2004 Presidential election to ensure that President Bush, a staunch defender of Israel and its policies, is re-elected to office.

DISSEMINATING MY BELIEFS TO OTHERS

8. On September, 11, 2001, just a couple of hours after the World Trade Center Towers in New York City collapsed, I began widely distributing my views that Israel and members of our own government loyal to Israel were responsible for the attacks. One of the first places where I expressed my beliefs was in an Internet discussion group (Zero Income Filers) located at Yahoo! Groups.com which was and still is comprised primarily of followers of my former income tax mentor, nationally-known income tax protester Irwin Schiff of Las Vegas, Nevada. According to the Government's own documents, this discussion group was being monitored by the Government at the time that I posted my messages regarding Israel's and others' complicity in the attacks. I shall provide evidence of that fact further on in this motion.

9. The first e-mail posting I sent to the Zero Income Filers (ZIF) discussion group expressing my beliefs was at 12:24 p.m. on September, 11, 2001 (Exhibit 1) I followed that

posting up a little while later that same day with another one. (Exhibit 2)

10. As I mentioned earlier, the Government has admitted that it was monitoring ZIF at the time of the September 11, 2001 terrorist attacks. ZIF was a discussion group set up to only discuss the income tax theories of Irwin Schiff and methods to legally stop paying income taxes using those theories. However, quite often group members would post statements to the group which had nothing to do with income taxes. As a way to prevent that from happening, the ZIF group owner began another discussion group at Yahoo! Groups.com entitled Zero Income Talk (ZIT) where members could have conversations on subjects other than income taxes.

11. Between the day of the terrorist attacks (September 11, 2001) and the day when I.R.S. Special Agents executed the search warrants at my home and the U.S. Attorney informed me that I was the target of a criminal investigation (January 9, 2002), I had posted many messages to Zero Income Talk (ZIT) expressing my beliefs that Israel and members of our own government loyal to Israel had orchestrated the terrorist attacks. (I am not reproducing those messages here because I do not have proof that the Government was monitoring the Zero Income Talk discussion group at the time I posted the messages. However, I do have proof that the Government was monitoring other Yahoo! discussion groups I belonged to at that time. So I believe that it is safe to assume that the Government was also monitoring the Zero Income Talk discussion group as well and that it was well aware of the messages I was posting. If the Court would like copies of the messages I posted, I can provide them.) There were also many private e-mails between myself and others expressing those beliefs during that time period. If the Court wishes, I can provide copies of those e-mails as well.

12. On September 20, 2001, I sent a letter-to-the-editor of the <u>Union Leader</u> of Manchester, New Hampshire expressing my beliefs.(Exhibit 3)

13. Also on September 20, 2001, I posted a message to ZIF expressing my beliefs and including an article from the

American Free Press expressing similar beliefs. (Exhibit 4) I also sent the message to the owner of another Internet discussion group at Yahoo! Groups.com, ICE (Investigating Curious Evidence), where the owner of the group is the only one who posts messages to the group. The last page of the exhibit shows to whom I e-mailed the posting.

14. Also on September 20, 2001, I sent another message to ICE expressing my beliefs and including an article from the Web site www.thisiscyberia.com entitled "Was Israel Involved in the WTC and Pentagon Terror Attacks?" (Exhibit 5) Again, the last page of the exhibit shows to whom the e-mail was sent.

15. On September 24, 2001, I posted another message to ZIF. (Exhibit 6)

16. Also on September 24, 2001, I e-mailed a letter-to-the-editor to The Weirs Times of Weirs Beach, New Hampshire expressing my views. (Exhibit 7)

17. On September 27, 2001, I e-mailed a letter to United States Senator Robert C. Smith from New Hampshire expressing my views. (Exhibit 8)

18. On October 8, 2001, I sent a letter-to-the-editor expressing my views to a number of local and regional newspapers. (Exhibit 9)

19. On October 26, 2001, I widely distributed via e-mail a story from the Internet Web site What Really Happened.com (www.whatreallyhappened.com) entitled "Are Americans the Victims of a Hoax?" to many news and opinion outlets. (Exhibits 10-A, 10-B, and 10-C) Again, the last pages of the exhibits show to whom the e-mails were sent.

20. On November 22, 2001, I e-mailed a letter-to-the-editor to the Union Leader of Manchester, New Hampshire expressing my views. (Exhibit 11)

21. On November 29, 2001, I e-mailed a letter-to-the-editor to The Weirs Times of Weirs Beach, New Hampshire expressing my views. (Exhibit 12)

22. On December 7, 2001, I e-mailed a letter-to-the-editor to the Union Leader of Manchester, New Hampshire expressing my views. (Exhibit 13)

23. That same day, I e-mail the same letter-to-the-editor to The Weirs Times of Weirs Beach, New Hampshire. (Exhibit 14)

24. On December 24, 2001, I e-mailed a letter-to-the-editor to the Union Leader of Manchester, New Hampshire expressing my views. (Exhibit 15)

25. On December 28, 2001, I widely distributed an opinion piece I authored entitled "How Long Will the News Media Allow Itself to Be Manipulated and Duped?" (Exhibit 16. I e-mailed this piece in a number of separate e-mails. Rather than reproduce each e-mail I sent out, I have only included the initial e-mail that I sent out along with the lists of everyone I sent the e-mail to as recorded by my e-mail messaging program. If the Court wishes, I can supply copies of each individual e-mail.)

26. On December 29, 2001, I widely distributed the transcript of a message from Dr. William Pierce of the National Alliance of Hillsboro, West Virginia in which he reproduces transcripts of reports from Fox News about Israeli espionage against the United States and about Israel's complicity in the September 11, 2001 terrorist attacks. (Exhibit 17. Again, rather than reproduce each e-mail I sent out, I have only included the initial e-mail that I sent out along with the lists of everyone I sent the e-mail to. If the Court wishes, I can supply copies of each individual e-mail.) In his message, Dr. Pierce contends that Fox News was forced to remove the reports from its Web site because there was such an outcry from Jews who were concerned that the reports might fuel anti-Semitism. (Just over a year ago, Dr. Pierce died unexpectedly at his home.)

27. On December 30, 2001, I widely distributed an e-mail providing Internet Web site addresses where people could read the reports critical of Israel which Fox News was forced to remove from its Web site. (Exhibit 18. Again, rather than reproduce each e-mail I sent out, I have only included the initial e-mail that I sent out along with the lists of everyone I sent the e-mail to. If the Court wishes, I can supply each individual e-mail.) I have also included copies of those Fox News reports here. (Exhibit 19)

28. Ten days later, on January 9, 2002, I.R.S. Special Agents executed search warrants at my home and provided me with a letter from the U.S. Attorney for the District of New Hampshire informing me that I was the target of a criminal investigation, which ultimately led to the charges I now face here.

29. After the Government searched my home and informed me that I was the target of a criminal investigation, I continued widely-distributing my beliefs that Israel and others loyal to Israel were responsible for the September 11, 2001 terrorist attacks. On March 5, 2003, the Government was successful in convincing a federal grand jury to indict me on eighteen (18) felony counts of violations of the internal revenue laws.

THE GOVERNMENT WAS MONITORING THE INTERNET DISCUSSION GROUPS TO WHICH I WAS POSTING MESSAGES

30. According to the Application and Affidavit for Search Warrant of Internal Revenue Service (I.R.S.) Special Agent Roberta J. Keenan in this case and executed by Magistrate Judge Muirhead on January 8, 2002 (Case Number 02-02M-01), Special Agent Keenan "began investigating [my] activities in or about September 1999."

31. According to the documents the Government provided to me during discovery in this case, the Internal Revenue Service requested a Grand Jury investigation into my activities on March 2, 2000. (Exhibit 20. They were Bates stamped with the numbers SUSAO-00003 through SUSAO-00005 prior to being disclosed to me on May 15, 2003.)

32. I am not sure when Assistant U.S. Attorney (AUSA) William E. Morse (the Assistant U.S. Attorney who is currently handling my case in conjunction with the U.S. Department of Justice's Tax Division in Washington, D.C.) began handling the Government's investigation of my activities, but one of the discovery documents disclosed to me by AUSA Morse was an envelope marked "US v Steven Swan 2000R00201 Sealed Document Tax Information." Inside the envelope was a form entitled "Safeguarding Tax Returns . . ." (Bates stamp number SUSAO—01325.) (I did

not make a copy of that document, but I will request one from AUSA Morse.) The form stated that it was received in the U.S. Attorney's Office on 8/10/00; that it was received by the Assistant U.S. Attorney on 8/10/00; and that the "Location of Same" was with the Swan case file in Attorney Morse's locked file cabinet.

33. Another discovery item disclosed to me by the Government on May 15, 2003 was a 3-ring binder containing six hundred fifty (650) pages of e-mail postings to the Zero Income Filers (ZIF) discussion group mentioned earlier (SUSAO-00703 through SUSAO-01313). The existence of these postings clearly indicates that the Government was monitoring this group. (I do not have copies of the first and last pages of the postings, but I do have copies of SUSAO-00721 [dated January 29, 2001] [Exhibit 21A] and SUSAO-01250 [dated January 4, 2001] [Exhibit 21B]. The date at the lower right corner of the page indicates the date the Government printed the posting from the discussion group Web site [1/29/02 and 1/30/01, respectively]. To the best of my recollection, all 650 pages of postings were from January of 2001. This was many months prior to the September 11, 2001 terrorist attacks and my postings about Israel's and others' complicity in those attacks.)

34. Another set of discovery items which the Government disclosed to me on July 3, 2003 were copies of e-mail postings it had of another Internet discussion group located at E-Groups.com dedicated solely to discussing the income tax theories of Irwin Schiff. That discussion group is entitled Tax-Freedom-Now (TFN). (Tax-Freedom-Now is now located at Yahoo! Groups, as are the other discussion groups I mentioned earlier. E-Groups was bought by Yahoo! Groups a number of years ago.) The postings which the Government has are ones I made in conversation with others in 1999. (Exhibit 22A [Bates stamped by the Government SUSAO-03898 through SUSAO-03903] and Exhibit 22B [Bates stamped by the Government SUSAO-03907]) The existence of these copies in the Government's possession shows that the Government was well aware of and probably monitoring the Tax-Freedom-Now discussion group as well as the other groups.

35. Another private e-mail in the Government's possession between me and another person was sandwiched between (as evidenced by the Bates stamp numbers) the two previously mentioned postings to the Tax-Freedom-Now group. (Exhibit 23, Bates stamped SUSAO-03904 through SUSAO-03906.) These conversations transpired between November 27, 2001 and December 5, 2001. This was during the time when I was extremely vocal about my views about Israel's and others' involvement in the terrorist attacks and approximately a month before the I.R.S. executed the search warrants at my home. This shows that the Government was monitoring my private e-mail messages as well as my postings to the discussion groups.

36. Another set of discovery items which the Government disclosed to me on September 9, 2003 were copies of one hundred forty-eight (148) pages of e-mail messages (SUSAO-010650 through SUSAO-010798) which I had posted to the previously-mentioned Zero Income Filers (ZIF), Tax-Freedom-Now (TFN), and Investigating Curious Evidence (ICE) discussion groups. This set of discovery items also included e-mail messages I had posted to another Internet discussion group at Yahoo! Groups.com called the We The People—Legality of Income Tax Group. The members of this group discuss many different theories about the federal income tax, including Irwin Schiff's theories. I am submitting copies of e-mails I posted to the We The People—Legality of Income Tax Group and the Investigating Curious Evidence (ICE) Group to show that the Government was aware of and probably monitoring these two discussion groups, as well as the ones from which I previously provided e-mail copies. (Exhibit 24A from the We The People—Legality-of-Income-Tax group [SUSAO-010650—SUSAO-010651] and Exhibit 24B from the Investigating Curious Evidence (ICE) Group [SUSAO-010746—SUSAO-010750]) The fact that the Government was aware of and monitoring these Internet discussion groups suggests that the Government was probably also aware of and monitoring the Zero Income Talk (ZIT) discussion group mentioned earlier where I posted a large number of e-mail messages about my beliefs prior to the I.R.S. executing the search warrants at my home.

The Government Also Possesses Copies Of My Published Letters Regarding My Beliefs

37. Another set of discovery items which the Government disclosed to me were copies in its possession of letters-to-the-editor authored by me about my beliefs regarding the terrorist attacks and which were published in various newspapers. On May 15, 2003, the Government disclosed to me that it had in its possession a copy of a letter written by me and published in the June 20, 2002 edition of <u>Bedford</u> (New Hampshire) <u>Journal</u>. (Exhibit 25 [SUSAO-01362]) The caption which the newspaper placed above my letter was "Cover-up?". On September 9, 2003, the Government disclosed to me that it possessed a copy of a letter written by me and published in the October 15, 2001 edition of <u>The Citizen</u> of Laconia, New Hampshire. (Exhibit 26 [SUSAO-010119]) The caption which the newspaper placed above that letter was "He blames the Israelis." Please take notice of the fact that this letter was published almost three (3) months before the I.R.S. executed the search warrants at my home. The existence of these letters in the Government's possession is evidence that the Government was interested in my writings about my beliefs regarding the September 11, 2001 terrorist attacks.

THE GOVERNMENT'S DECISION TO PROSECUTE ME WAS MADE ON A SELECTIVE AND VINDICTIVE BASIS

38. On January 9, 2002, the I.R.S. executed two (2) search warrants against me at my home and the U.S. Attorney for the District of New Hampshire informed me that I was the target of a criminal investigation for alleged violations of the internal revenue laws. On March 5, 2003, the Government was successful in convincing a federal grand jury to indict me on eighteen (18) counts of alleged violations of the internal revenue laws, which it did. However my former mentor, nationally-known income tax protester Irwin Schiff, was much more highly-visible than I was and, by his own account, up to one (1) million Americans have stopped paying federal income taxes based upon his income tax theories. So why hasn't Schiff nor any of his other followers been prosecuted by the Government for violations of the internal revenue laws? Because this is not a case about the

federal income tax; it is a case about silencing a person who is exposing Israel's and others loyal to Israel's involvement in the September 11, 2001 terrorist attacks against the United States.

THE GOVERNMENT WAS WELL AWARE OF IRWIN SCHIFF AND HIS INCOME TAX ACTIVITIES

The Activities of Irwin A. Schiff

39. For approximately the last twenty-five (25) years, Irwin A. Schiff of Las Vegas, Nevada has been challenging the legality of the federal income tax laws, advising Americans that anyone can legally stop paying federal income taxes, and encouraging anyone who would listen to him to "legally" stop paying federal income taxes using his procedures and methods.

40. Mr. Schiff has been conducting these activities through books he has written, e.g., *How Anyone Can Stop Paying Income Taxes* (1982); *The Great Income Tax Hoax* (1985); and *The Federal Mafia: How It Illegally Imposes and Unlawfully Collects Income Taxes* (1990); through his well-publicized political campaign in 1995 and 1996 to become President of the United States as the candidate from the Libertarian Party in the 1996 Presidential election; through his Internet Web site www.paynoincometax.com (Pay No Income Tax.com); through his business, Freedom Books, located at 444 East Sahara Avenue, in Las Vegas, Nevada; through his radio talk show in Las Vegas, Nevada, which was also broadcast over short-wave radio, by satellite, and over the Internet; through countless income tax seminars he has conducted all over the United States; through video-tapes and audio-tapes of his seminars; through audio-tape updates to the books he has written (the Schiff Audio Reports); through extensive commercial advertising he has purchased; and through numerous television, radio, newspaper, and magazine interviews he has granted.

The Government Was Well Aware of Schiff's Activities

41. For many years the Government did very little to attempt to enjoin Schiff from promoting his income tax theories and from encouraging Americans to "legally" stop paying federal income taxes. On April 6, 1995 (shortly after

Schiff moved to Las Vegas, Nevada), Special Agents of the Internal Revenue Service (I.R.S.) confronted Schiff in his automobile. Schiff resisted the I.R.S. agents' attempt to confiscate his vehicle and he was pepper-sprayed and arrested. However, the I.R.S. subsequently dropped any charges it had filed against Schiff. To my knowledge, the only other time (until relatively recently) that the I.R.S. had attempted to force Schiff to comply with the internal revenue laws was on August 11, 1999, when Schiff was summoned to produce his books and records at an I.R.S. audit at the I.R.S. offices in Las Vegas, Nevada. After nearly two hours of interaction between Schiff and the I.R.S. agents who were attempting to audit him, Schiff refused to produce his books and records and no further action was taken by the I.R.S. or the Justice Department against Schiff. Schiff subsequently included an audio recording of this audit interview in his Schiff Audio Reports, Series 6, Tapes 1 and 2. He used it as an example to his followers of how to handle an I.R.S. audit and to prove to them that the I.R.S. has no authority to audit a person's books and records and that nothing would happen to them if they refused to produce their books and records.

42. Then on August 2, 2001, the U.S. Department of Justice filed a civil action against Schiff in U.S. District Court for Nevada to reduce to judgment assessments made against Schiff in the amount of approximately $2.3 million. The case is docketed as Case Number CV-S-01-0895-PMP-LRL. However, as unbelievable as it may sound, the Government was only attempting to collect federal income taxes, penalties and interest from Schiff for tax years 1979 through 1985, inclusive! The Government took no other legal action to attempt to collect taxes from Schiff for any other tax years, nor did it attempt to enjoin Schiff from promoting his income tax theories and from encouraging others to challenge the legality of the federal income tax laws. Furthermore, the Government has not prosecuted Schiff for his income tax-related activities. For many years Schiff touted the Government's inaction against him as proof that his assertions about the federal income tax being entirely voluntary were correct.

43. On March 12, 2003, the U.S. Department of Justice filed a Complaint for Permanent Injunction and Other Relief against Schiff and his associates, Cynthia Neun and Lawrence Cohen, in U.S. District Court for the District of Nevada in Las Vegas. The case is docketed as Case Number CV-S-03-0281-LDG-RJJ. The Complaint is Docket Entry # 1.

44. Some of the assertions made by the Government in its complaint against Schiff which prove that it was well aware of Schiff's activities over many years are as follows:

Schiff prepares, promotes, and markets improper tax-avoidance schemes purporting to exempt his customers from federal income taxation and advertising how to frustrate the Government's attempts to ascertain customers' taxable income, assess taxes, and collect against assets. Schiff has promoted abusive tax schemes since at least the 1970's. (Government's Complaint at ¶ 8.)

Schiff has admitted that he has not made any voluntary federal-income-tax payments since 1973, despite receiving substantial income generated by his books, seminars, and tape sales from at least 1973 to the present. (Government's Complaint at ¶ 9.)

Schiff's income-tax theories have been rejected in numerous civil suits involving Schiff's non-payment of taxes in Tax Court and federal district and appellate courts. Schiff's theories have been rejected every time, and the courts have imposed against him sanctions of up to $25,000 for repeatedly raising frivolous arguments. (Government's Complaint at ¶ 11.)

Neun [an associate of Schiff] claims that Schiff has "over a million students following his research . . . " (Government's Complaint at ¶ 16.)

Neun has continually and repeatedly prepared fraudulent federal income tax returns as a paid return preparer, including Schiff's 1996 through 2001 tax returns. (Government's Complaint at ¶ 26.)

The IRS estimates that, based on a random sampling of Schiff's 3100 identified customers, the total amount of taxes that Schiff's customers have evaded or attempted to evade is $56,000,000 for tax years 1999 through 2001. Because

Schiff has been selling his tax schemes since at least 1994, the total amount of taxes that Schiff's customers have evaded or attempted to evade likely is much higher. (Government's Complaint at ¶ 32.)

45. In the same action against Schiff and his associates, the Government also filed a Motion and Memorandum in Support of Motion for Temporary Restraining Order and for Preliminary Injunction. (Docket Entry # 4.) Some of the assertions made against Schiff by the Government in its Motion and Memorandum in Support of its motion which also prove that it was well aware of Schiff's activities over many years are as follows:

The IRS has identified nearly 5,000 frivolous "zero-income" returns filed by some 3,100 customers of Schiff, Neun, and/or Cohen during the past three years, amounting to an estimated $56 million in attempted tax evasion. (footnote omitted.) (Government's Motion at 2.)

Schiff—a longtime tax protestor and purveyor of tax schemes who has twice been convicted of tax crimes—has been selling tax-scam materials since the 1970's and holding tax-evasion seminars since at least the mid-1990s, after serving out his last prison sentence. (footnote omitted.) Schiff claims that he has paid no income taxes since 1973 and has filed "zero income" tax returns—showing zero income and zero tax liability—since at least 1990. (footnote omitted.) Schiff admitted in 2002 on the Fox News television show *Hannity and Colmes* that he has earned "plenty" of income during the years in which he filed zero income returns. (footnote omitted.) (Government's Motion at 3.)

Schiff claims that "[h]undreds of thousands (if not millions) of Americans no longer pay income taxes because of the information contained in his books." (footnote omitted.) The IRS has identified 3,100 Schiff customers who have evaded or attempted to evade approximately $56 million in tax in the past three years. (footnote omitted.) (Government's Motion at 3.)

46. Even though it is obvious from the Government's own pleading and filings in this case that the Government is well aware of the fact that Schiff has been convincing otherwise unsuspecting Americans for many years that the federal

income tax laws are a "fraud" and that anyone can "legally" stop paying them, the Government has only recently attempted to enjoin Schiff from promoting his income tax theories and it has yet to prosecute Schiff for obvious violations of the internal revenue laws. In addition, to my knowledge the Government has not prosecuted any other Schiff followers other than myself, or if it has, it has only prosecuted a very small number of them. This fact tends to bolster my claim that I am the victim of a selective and vindictive prosecution by the Government for expressing my views rather than because of my income tax activities.

47. Furthermore, it is a common practice for the Justice Department to prosecute lesser-known figures in what it perceives to be criminal enterprises in order to coerce those figures into assisting the Government in its investigation of more highly-placed figures. However, the strategy of prosecuting me in order to coerce me into testifying against Irwin Schiff would not have been productive against Schiff because Schiff has never made any attempt to hide any of his income tax theories or income tax activities and to this day he still firmly believes his theories are correct and he still encourages others to use them. (Even though the U.S. District Court in Nevada issued an injunction against Schiff and enjoined him from promoting his income tax theories (CV-03-281-LDG), the Ninth Circuit Court of Appeals has granted a stay of that injunction (Case No. 03-16319) and Schiff is still promoting his income tax theories and selling his materials and advising people that they can legally stop paying federal income taxes.)

48. As further proof that the Government was aware of Irwin Schiff and his income tax activities, on May 15, 2003, the Government disclosed to me two hundred eighteen (218) pages of court cases involving or mentioning Irwin Schiff. These cases are Bates stamped numbered from SUSAO-00169 through SUSAO-00387.

My Actions May Have Been Responsible for the Government's Decision to Attempt to Enjoin Schiff's Income Tax Activities

49. After I realized that Irwin Schiff's theories about the federal income tax were incorrect, I wrote letters to the

Attorney General of the United States and the Commissioner of Internal Revenue on August 8, 2002 asking why the Government had not prosecuted Schiff or attempted to enjoin him from disseminating his erroneous income tax theories. (Exhibit 27, Attorney General letter) On January 15, 2003, I also wrote letters to Government officials about my concern that certain Government employees were purposely allowing Schiff to remain in business so that the I.R.S. could collect more money in taxes, penalties, and interest than it would otherwise be able to collect and for other reasons. I wrote these letters to President Bush, to Attorney General Ashcroft, to the Department of Justice Inspector General, to the Secretary of the Treasury, to the Treasury Inspector General for Tax Administration, to the Senate Finance Committee (which has oversight over I.R.S. activities), to Congress' Joint Committee on Taxation, to the House Government Reform Committee, and to my U.S. Senators and Congressman (Gregg, Sununu, and Bradley). (A copy of the letter I sent to the Attorney General to the United States can be found in this case at Exhibit B of my Motion to Dismiss the Superceding [sic] Indictment Against Me Because of the Government's Complicity in My Actions. (Doc. # 37)

50. The next day, I also e-mailed a copy of the letter I sent to President Bush to much of the national and local news media. The e-mail I issued was entitled "Open Letter Regarding Justice Department and Internal Revenue Service Malfeasance." And on February 1, 2003, I sent out a number of letters-to-the-editor about this issue, one of which was published by the *New Hampshire Sunday News* of Manchester, New Hampshire in its February 16, 2003 issue. (Id at Exhibit C)

51. I do not know if my letters to Government officials, my press releases, or my letters-to-the-editor had anything to do with it, but on February 11, 2003, I.R.S. Special Agents executed a search warrant at Schiff's Las Vegas, Nevada office and informed Schiff that he was the target of a federal grand jury investigation for possible violations of the internal revenue laws. John L. Smith, <u>Maybe if Schiff, allies repeat fiction long enough, it will become fact</u>, Las Vegas Review-Journal, February 19, 2003, online article. Who knows, if I

had not issued those letters, press releases and letters-to-the-editor, the Government still might not have decided to attempt to enjoin Schiff or otherwise investigate him to this day.

52. Further evidence that the Government was well aware of Schiff's activities can be found in the "Application and Affidavit for Search Warrant" of Internal Revenue Service (I.R.S.) Special Agent Roberta J. Keenan, which led to the search warrants which were executed against me. In paragraph 23 of her affidavit, Special Agent Keenan states "SWAN takes his income tax theories, almost in their entirety, from Irwin Schiff . . ." And in the section of her affidavit captioned "Items to Be Seized", in paragraph g she lists "documents relating to Irwin Schiff, dated during, or pertaining to, the period January 1, 1996, to the present;" This statement is restated in the actual Search Warrant itself in paragraph g of Attachment B. Remember that this search warrant was applied for and executed in January of 2002. Yet in the almost two years since then, the Government still has not prosecuted Irwin Schiff for violations of the internal revenue laws. However, it is prosecuting me.

53. The Court should keep in mind (as printed in paragraph 44 above) the Government's assertion that—

The IRS has identified nearly 5,000 frivolous "zero-income" returns filed by some 3,100 customers of Schiff, Neun, and/or Cohen during the past three years, amounting to an estimated $56 million in attempted tax evasion. (footnote omitted.) (Government's Motion at 2.)

However, these are only "zero-income" tax returns directly attributable to customers of Schiff, Neun, and/or Cohen during the past three years. Since Schiff published his latest book, The Federal Mafia, thirteen years ago and since he has over 400,000 of his books informing Americans that they can legally stop paying federal income taxes in circulation, the number of people following Schiff's methods probably is in the hundreds of thousands. However, I am the only one of Schiff's many followers being prosecuted by the Justice Department. Even Schiff himself has not been prosecuted. One would think that if the Government were truly interested in prosecuting people for filing tax returns using Irwin Schiff's methods, it would have prosecuted Irwin Schiff first. This is further evidence of the fact that I am the victim of a selective and vindictive prosecution by the Government for expressing my beliefs. And this does not even take into consideration all of the other promoters of arguments and schemes against the federal income tax other than Schiff and all of the followers of those arguments and schemes who the Government is neglecting to prosecute. Some of these other arguments and schemes can be found on the I.R.S.' Web site located at www.irs.gov.

THE GOVERNMENT WAS WELL AWARE THAT MANY OTHER AMERICANS WERE AND ARE USING SCHIFF'S THEORIES TO STOP PAYING FEDERAL INCOME TAXES

54. I showed earlier in this motion that the Government was well aware of and monitoring Internet discussion groups who subscribe to Irwin Schiff's theories about the federal income tax. There are many Americans who belong to these Schiff discussion groups and they are quite active in discussing and promoting Schiff's income tax theories. For instance, on October 9, 2003, I printed out the Home Page of the Tax-Freedom-Now discussion group. (Exhibit 28) The description of the group specifically states that it is dedicated to the discussion of Irwin Schiff's income tax methods. This page also shows that the group was founded on January 24, 1999 and that as of that date it had one thousand thirty-eight (1538) members. Page 2 of the printout shows that since the group was founded there have been forty-three thousand, four hundred twenty-nine (43,429) separate e-mail messages to the group. This represents quite a few conversations about Irwin Schiff's income tax theories. However, I am the only one of Schiff's many followers to be prosecuted.

55. That same day, I printed out the Home Page of the Zero Income Filers discussion group. (Exhibit 29) This page begins with a photograph of Irwin Schiff in the "Description" section. The Home Page states that this group was founded on February 17, 2000 and that as of the date of the print-out, it had six hundred sixty-seven (667) members. This page also shows that since the group was founded there have been thirty-two thousand, six hundred fifty-eight (32,658) separate e-mail messages to the group. Again, this

represents a lot of people discus-sing how to use Irwin Schiff's income tax methods. Yet, I am the only one of Schiff's many followers who the Government has seen fit to prosecute. This is because my prosecution has nothing to do with income taxes; the only reason I am being prosecuted is because I exercised my right to free speech and expression and criticized and exposed a very powerful world entity— Israel and those loyal to it, many of whom are high-ranking officials in our own Government.

THE U.S. ATTORNEY FOR NEW HAMPSHIRE IS PROSECUTING ME IN CONJUNCTION WITH THE U.S. DEPARTMENT OF JUSTICE IN WASHINGTON, D.C.

56. I do not believe that the decision to selectively and vindictively prosecute me originated in the New Hampshire U.S. Attorney's Office. Rather, I believe that the decision to selectively and vindictively prosecute me either originated with the Justice Department in Washington, D.C. or with some person or persons higher up in the Bush Administration. I believe that the Assistant Attorney General for the Criminal Division of the U.S. Department of Justice, Michael Chertoff, is Jewish and a dual-loyalist to both the United States and Israel. In his capacity, Mr. Chertoff has the ability to ensure that anyone who criticizes Israel and those within our own government who are loyal to Israel are prosecuted. For example, in 2002 former Louisiana state congressman and former U.S. Presidential candidate David Duke author-ed a book entitled "Jewish Supremacism." Shortly thereafter, Duke was indicted on trumped up charges of tax evasion (U.S. v. Duke, E.D. Louisiana, Case # 02-CR-345-ALL), to which he pleaded guilty rather than risk being sentenced to even more time in prison if he fought the charges and lost. And in another recent case, former German and former Canadian citizen, Ernst Zundel (who is well-known because he raises questions regarding certain facets of the Holocaust), was arrested at his home in Tennessee by the U.S. Government and deported to Canada, even though he is legally married to an American citizen. His wife brought suit in the Eastern District of Tennessee to halt her husband's illegal deportation and she then appealed to the Sixth Circuit Court of Appeals (Case # 03-5212), but to no avail. I am sure that there are many more examples of

people being prosecuted or deported because they criticized or questioned certain facets pertaining to Israel or to Jewish causes in general. It is apparent that certain members of the U.S. Government have no qualms about prosecuting or deporting anyone who engages in this activity. I do not possess any concrete evidence that Assistant Attorney General Chertoff was instrumental in the decision to prosecute me. There are probably many other Jews who are dual-loyalists to both the United States and Israel in the Criminal Division of the Justice Department or within the Justice Department or the federal Government as a whole who could have made the decision to prosecute me. To ascertain who made the decision to selectively and vindictively prosecute me is a reason as to why an evidentiary hearing into this matter is necessary.

The U.S. Department of Justice Is Intimately Involved in My Prosecution

57. Evidence that the U.S. Department of Justice in Washington, D.C. is intimately involved in my prosecution can be found in the Media Release issued by the U.S. Attorney for New Hampshire on March 10, 2003. (Exhibit 30) The caption of the release states "Auburn Tax Return Preparer Indicted." The last sentence of the release states—

This matter was investigated by special agents of the Internal Revenue Service and is being prosecuted by Assistant U.S. Attorney Bill Morse and James W. Chapman, a Trial Attorney with the U.S. Department of Justice, Tax Division.

58. Further proof that the U.S. Department of Justice in Washington, D.C. is involved in prosecuting me is contained in the Government's Opposition to [My] Motion to Dismiss Indictment Based on Claim that the Tax Laws Are Unconstitutional filed with this Court on August 1, 2002. (Doc. # 50) That document was submitted by both New Hampshire Assistant U.S. Attorney William E. Morse and by Trial Attorney James W. Chapman, Jr., who is with the U.S. Department of Justice's Tax Division in Washington, D.C. Furthermore, on August 11, 2003, I received an undated latter from Attorney Chapman from his office in Washington, D.C. (Exhibit 31) The first sentence of that letter states "I

am prosecuting your case along with Assistant U.S. Attorney Morse."

59. The fact that the Justice Department is intimately involved in my prosecution is further evidence that I am being selectively and vindictively prosecuted by the Government for expressing my beliefs.

BECAUSE I HAVE EXPOSED AND CRITICISED EXTREMELY POWERFUL INTERESTS, I HAVE EXPRESSED CONCERNS FOR MY LIFE

60. Once I realized that I was being vindictively and selectively prosecuted by the U.S. Government for alleging that Israel and those loyal to Israel were responsible of the September 11, 2001 terrorist attacks against the United States and that I intended to vigorously defend my-self in this Court by filing this motion, I realized that my life might be in danger because these interests are extremely powerful and they permeate nearly every facet of our society. So I wrote letters to the President of the United States, the Attorney General of the United States and many other officials expressing my concerns for my life in the hope of circumventing any attacks against me by these extremely powerful interests. I am including a copy of my letter to President Bush here. (Exhibit 32) As another method of attempting to circumvent any retaliation against me, I also e-mailed my concerns and a copy of my letter to President Bush to as many media outlets as I could think of.

AN EVIDENTIARY HEARING INTO THIS MATTER IS NECESSARY

61. The Court should order an evidentiary hearing into this matter so that the Court and I might attempt to ascertain answers to the following questions and others pertinent to this matter:

a. Whether or nor I was vindictively and selectively prosecuted by the Government for expressing my rights of free speech and expression under the First Amendment to the Constitution of the United States;

b. Who made the determination to institute the Grand Jury investigation of me and when and on what basis was the determination made?

c. Who made the determination to apply for and execute the search warrants against me and when and on what basis was the determination made?

d. Who made the determination to request the Grand Jury to indict me and when and on what basis was the determination made?

e. Why I was selected for prosecution when neither Irwin Schiff nor any of his other thousands of followers was selected for prosecution?

f. Were there any inconsistencies in the timing of the events in my prosecution as compared to other prosecutions?

g. Was the Government monitoring my e-mail postings in the Zero Income Talk discussion group regarding my beliefs about Israel's and others' complicity in the September 11, 2001 terrorist attacks?

h. Was the Government monitoring my other e-mail messages regarding my beliefs about Israel's and others' complicity in the September 11, 2001 terrorist attacks?

i. Did my letters to Government officials have anything to do with the Government's decision to finally attempt to enjoin Irwin Schiff from disseminating his income tax theories to others and to investigate him criminally?

These questions and others should be asked of Internal Revenue Service employees, U.S. Attorney's Office employees, and U.S. Department of Justice employees who were involved in any way with this case in an attempt to ascertain whether or not I have been selectively and vindictively prosecuted by the Government for expressing my beliefs.

WHEREFORE, I respectfully request that this Court—

>A. Order an evidentiary hearing into this matter so that the Court and I might examine all Government employees involved in my prosecution in an attempt to ascertain whether I have been vindictively and/or selectively prosecuted by the Government for exercising my right to free speech and expression under the First Amendment to the Constitution of the United States; or

B. Order the Government to provide me with discovery so that I might procure more evidence to bolster my assertions; or, in the alternative,

C. Dismiss the charges against me because I am the victim of a selective and/or vindictive prosecution by the Government for exercising my right to free speech and expression under the First Amendment to the Constitution of the United States; and

D. State its essential findings with respect to factual issues on the record; and

E. Provide such other and further relief as is authorized by law or equity.

A memorandum in support of this motion is included with it. An Affidavit is included with the separately-bound exhibits. The Government has been contacted and it does not concur with this motion.

Dated: October 13, 2003   Respectfully submitted,

Steven A. Swan, pro se

My motion included thirty-two (32) exhibits pertinent to why I believed that I was being vindictively and/or selectively prosecuted. Here is the Table of Contents of the Exhibits: (Most of these Exhibits have already been reproduced in this book.)

TABLE OF CONTENTS

Exhibits   Description

A. Affidavit

1. September 11, 2001 E-Mail Posting to ZIF

2. September 11, 2001 E-Mail Posting to ZIF

3. September 20, 2001 Letter to the Editor—Union Leader

4. September 20, 2001 E-Mail to ZIF and ICE

5. September 20, 2001 E-Mail to ICE

6. September 24, 2001 E-Mail Posting to ZIF

7. September 24, 2001 Letter to the Editor—Weirs Times

8. September 27, 2001 Letter to U.S. Senator Smith

9. October 8, 2001 Letter to the Editor—Various Newspapers

10A. October 26, 2001 E-Mail of Article

10B. October 26, 2001 E-Mail of Article

10C. October 26, 2001 E-Mail of Article

11. November 22, 2001 Letter to the Editor—Union Leader

12. November 29, 2001 Letter to the Editor—Weirs Times

13. December 7, 2001 Letter to the Editor—Union Leader

14. December 7, 2001 Letter to the Editor—Weirs Times

15. December 24, 2001 Letter to the Editor—Union Leader

16. December 28, 2001 Opinion Piece E-Mail

17. December 29, 2001 Dr. William Pierce Article E-Mail

18. December 30, 2001 E-Mail—Links to Fox News Articles

19. Fox News Articles

20. Grand Jury Investigation Request

21A. January 29, 2001 Posting to ZIF

21B. January 4, 2001 Posting to ZIF

22A. TFN E-Mails—C. Casey

22B. TFN E-Mails—B.Watts

23. Harley Oakes E-Mails

24A. We the People—Legality of Income Tax E-Mail

24B. ICE Posts

25. June 20, 2002 Letter to the Editor—Bedford Journal

26. October 15, 2001 Letter to the Editor—The Citizen, Laconia, N.H.

27. August 8, 2002 Letter to the Attorney General of the United States

28. Tax-Freedom-Now Home Page

29. Zero Income Filers Home Page

30. March 10, 2003 Press Release from U.S. Attorney Colantuono

31. Letter from U.S. Department of Justice Trial Attorney Chapman

32. September 7, 2003 Letter to President Bush

The following is a copy of the sworn affidavit I filed in conjunction with my motion. I was swearing to the veracity of factual statements I made in my motion. Again, I am reproducing the affidavit in plain text after the copy so that it can be read by anyone using any device.

UNITED STATES DISTRICT COURT
FOR THE DISTRICT OF NEW HAMPSHIRE

UNITED STATES OF AMERICA)
    Plaintiff)
       v.)   Criminal No. 03-36-01-B
)
STEVEN A. SWAN)
    Defendant)
_____)

AFFIDAVIT

Steven A. Swan, being first duly sworn, deposes and says:

1. I am the Defendant in the above-captioned proceeding. This affidavit is submitted in conjunction with my motion to dismiss the charges against me because I am being selectively and vindictively prosecuted by the Government.

2. For many years, I have been an outspoken critic of what I perceive to be corruption by federal government officials and the manipulation of those officials by wealthy and powerful members of special interest groups.

3. Over the years, I have employed many different methods to disseminate my criticism of those government officials and special interest groups.

4. Some of the high-ranking federal government officials of whom I have been highly critical over the years have been Jews who seem to have a dual loyalty to both the United States and Israel.

5. After the September 11, 2001 terrorist attacks against the United States, I pondered who might have been responsible for them and who might have benefited the most from them.

6. I came to the conclusion that Israel and high-ranking dual-loyalists to Israel within our own Government were responsible for the attacks.

7. The Zero Income Filers Internet discussion group was and still is comprised primarily of followers of my former income tax mentor, nationally-known income tax protester Irwin Schiff of Las Vegas, Nevada.

8. Zero Income Talk was another Internet discussion group set up by the owner of the Zero Income Filers discussion group where members could have conversations on subjects other than income taxes.

EXHIBIT A

9. Between the day of the terrorist attacks (September 11, 2001) and the day when I.R.S. Special Agents executed the search warrants at my home and the U.S. Attorney informed me that I was the target of a criminal investigation (January 9, 2002), I had posted many messages to Zero Income Talk (ZIT) expressing my beliefs that Israel and members of our own government loyal to Israel had orchestrated the terrorist attacks.

10. There were also many private e-mails between myself and others expressing those beliefs during that time period.

11. Just over a year ago, Dr. William Pierce, the founder and head of a group called The National Alliance, died unexpectedly at his home.

12. After the Government executed the search warrants at my home and informed me that I was the target of a criminal investigation, I continued widely-distributing my beliefs that Israel and others loyal to Israel were responsible for the September 11, 2001 terrorist attacks.

13. One of the discovery items disclosed to me by the Government on May 15, 2003 was a 3-ring binder containing six hundred fifty (650) pages of e-mail postings to the Zero Income Filers (ZIF) discussion group mentioned earlier (SUSAO-00703 through SUSAO-01313).

14. To the best of my recollection, all 650 pages of postings were from January of 2001.

15. Another set of discovery items which the Government disclosed to me on September 9, 2003 were copies of one hundred forty-eight (148) pages of e-mail messages (SUSAO-010650 through SUSAO-010798) which I had posted to the Zero Income Filers (ZIF), Tax-Freedom-Now (TFN), and Investigating Curious Evidence (ICE) Internet discussion groups.

16. My belief is that I am not being prosecuted because of my income tax activities; I am being prosecuted for exposing Israel's and others loyal to Israel's involvement in the September 11, 2001 terrorist attacks against the United States.

17. For approximately the last twenty-five (25) years, Irwin A. Schiff of Las Vegas, Nevada has been challenging the legality of the federal income tax laws, advising Americans that anyone can legally stop paying federal income taxes, and encouraging anyone who would listen to him to "legally" stop paying federal income taxes using his procedures and methods.

18. Mr. Schiff has been conducting these activities through books he has written, e.g., *How Anyone Can Stop Paying Income Taxes* (1982); *The Great Income Tax Hoax* (1985); and *The Federal Mafia: How It Illegally Imposes and Unlawfully Collects Income Taxes* (1990); through his well-publicized political campaign in 1995 and 1996 to become President of the United States as the candidate from the Libertarian Party in the 1996 Presidential election; through his Internet Web site www.paynoincometax.com (Pay No Income Tax.com); through his business, Freedom Books, located at 444 East Sahara Avenue, in Las Vegas, Nevada; through his radio talk show in Las Vegas, Nevada, which was also broadcast over short-wave radio, by satellite, and over the Internet; through countless income tax seminars he has con-

ducted all over the United States; through video-tapes and audio-tapes of his seminars; through audio-tape updates to the books he has written (the Schiff Audio Reports); through extensive commercial advertising he has purchased; and through numerous television, radio, newspaper, and magazine interviews he has granted.

19. For many years the Government did very little to attempt to enjoin Schiff from promoting his income tax theories and from encouraging Americans to "legally" stop paying federal income taxes.

20. On April 6, 1995 (shortly after Schiff moved to Las Vegas, Nevada), Special Agents of the Internal Revenue Service (I.R.S.) confronted Schiff in his automobile. Schiff resisted the I.R.S. agents' attempt to confiscate his vehicle and he was pepper-sprayed and arrested. However, the I.R.S. subsequently dropped any charges it had filed against Schiff.

21. To my knowledge, the only other time (until relatively recently) that the I.R.S. had attempted to force Schiff to comply with the internal revenue laws was on August 11, 1999, when Schiff was summoned to produce his books and records at an I.R.S. audit at the I.R.S. offices in Las Vegas, Nevada. After nearly two hours of interaction between Schiff and the I.R.S. agents who were attempting to audit him, Schiff refused to produce his books and records and no further action was taken by the I.R.S. or the Justice Department against Schiff. Schiff subsequently included an audio recording of this audit interview in his Schiff Audio Reports, Series 6, Tapes 1 and 2. He used it as an example to his followers of how to handle an I.R.S. audit and to prove to them that the I.R.S. has no authority to audit a person's books and records and that nothing would happen to them if they refused to produce their books and records.

22. In its civil action against Schiff, the Government was only attempting to collect federal income taxes, penalties and interest from Schiff for tax years 1979 through 1985, inclusive! The Government took no other legal action to attempt to collect taxes from Schiff for any other tax years, nor did it attempt to enjoin Schiff from promoting his income tax theories and from encouraging others to challenge the legality of the federal income tax laws. Furthermore, the Government has not prosecuted Schiff for his income tax-related activities. For many years Schiff touted the Government's inaction against him as proof that his assertions about the federal income tax being entirely voluntary were correct.

23. To my knowledge, the Government has only recently attempted to enjoin Schiff from promoting his income tax theories and it has yet to prosecute Schiff for obvious violations of the internal revenue laws.

24. To my knowledge the Government has not prosecuted any other Schiff followers other than myself, or if it has, it has only prosecuted a very small number of them.

25. As further proof that the Government was aware of Irwin Schiff and his income tax activities, on May 15, 2003, the Government disclosed to me two hundred eighteen (218) pages of court cases involving or mentioning Irwin Schiff. These cases are Bates stamped numbered from SUSAO-00169 through SUSAO-00387.

26. On January 15, 2003, I wrote letters to Government officials about my concern that certain

3

Government employees were purposely allowing Schiff to remain in business so that the I.R.S. could collect more money in taxes, penalties, and interest than it would otherwise be able to collect and for other reasons.

27. The next day, I also e-mailed a copy of the letter I sent to President Bush to much of the national and local news media. The e-mail I issued was entitled "Open Letter Regarding Justice Department and Internal Revenue Service Malfeasance."

28. Schiff published his latest book, The Federal Mafia, thirteen years ago and he has over 400,000 of his books informing Americans that they can legally stop paying federal income taxes in circulation.

29. I believe that the decision to selectively and vindictively prosecute me either originated with the Justice Department in Washington, D.C. or with some person or persons higher up in the Bush Administration.

30. I believe that the Assistant Attorney General for the Criminal Division of the U.S. Department of Justice, Michael Chertoff, is Jewish and a dual-loyalist to both the United States and Israel.

31. In 2002 former Louisiana state congressman and former U.S. Presidential candidate David Duke authored a book entitled "Jewish Supremacism."

32. Former German and former Canadian citizen, Ernst Zundel (who is well-known because he raises questions regarding certain facets of the Holocaust), was arrested at his home in Tennessee by the U.S. Government and deported to Canada, even though he is legally married to an American citizen.

33. Once I realized that I was being vindictively and selectively prosecuted by the U.S. Government for alleging that Israel and those loyal to Israel were responsible of the September 11, 2001 terrorist attacks against the United States and that I intended to vigorously defend myself in this Court by filing this motion, I realized that my life might be in danger because these interests are extremely powerful and they permeate nearly every facet of our society.

34. So I wrote letters to the President of the United States, the Attorney General of the United States and many other officials expressing my concerns for my life in the hope of circumventing any attacks against me by these extremely powerful interests.

35. As another method of attempting to circumvent any retaliation against me, I also e-mailed my concerns and a copy of my letter to President Bush to as many media outlets as I could think of.

4

36. I understand that any false statements made in this affidavit will subject me to the penalties of perjury.

Steven A. Swan

Sworn to and subscribed before me this 14 day of October, 2003.

CHRISTINE M BOURGEOIS, Notary Public
My Commission Expires March 22, 2005

"UNITED STATES DISTRICT COURT
FOR THE DISTRICT OF NEW HAMPSHIRE

UNITED STATES OF AMERICA	)	
Plaintiff	)	Criminal No.
v.	)	03-36-01-B
STEVEN A. SWAN	)	
Defendant	)	
_____	)	

AFFIDAVIT

Steven A. Swan, being first duly sworn, deposes and says:

1. I am the Defendant in the above-captioned proceeding. This affidavit is submitted in conjunction with my motion to dismiss the charges against me because I am being selectively and vindictively prosecuted by the Government.

2. For many years, I have been an outspoken critic of what I perceive to be corruption by federal government officials and the manipulation of those officials by wealthy and powerful members of special interest groups.

3. Over the years, I have employed many different methods to disseminate my criticism of those government officials and special interest groups.

4. Some of the high-ranking federal government officials of whom I have been highly critical over the years have been Jews who seem to have a dual loyalty to both the United States and Israel.

5. After the September 11, 2001 terrorist attacks against the United States, I pondered who might have been responsible for them and who might have benefited the most from them.

6. I came to the conclusion that Israel and high-ranking dual-loyalists to Israel within our own Government were responsible for the attacks.

7. The Zero Income Filers Internet discussion group was and still is comprised primarily of followers of my former income tax mentor, nationally-known income tax protester Irwin Schiff of Las Vegas, Nevada.

8. Zero Income Talk was another Internet discussion group set up by the owner of the Zero Income Filers discussion group where members could have conversations on subjects other than income taxes.

9. Between the day of the terrorist attacks (September 11, 2001) and the day when I.R.S. Special Agents executed the search warrants at my home and the U.S. Attorney informed me that I was the target of a criminal investigation (January 9, 2002), I had posted many messages to Zero Income Talk (ZIT) expressing my beliefs that Israel and members of our own government loyal to Israel had orchestrated the terrorist attacks.

10. There were also many private e-mails between myself and others expressing those beliefs during that time period.

11. Just over a year ago, Dr. William Pierce, the founder and head of a group called The National Alliance, died unexpectedly at his home.

12. After the Government executed the search warrants at my home and informed me that I was the target of a criminal investigation, I continued widely-distributing my beliefs that Israel and others loyal to Israel were responsible for the September 11, 2001 terrorist attacks.

13. One of the discovery items disclosed to me by the Government on May 15, 2003 was a 3-ring binder containing six hundred fifty (650) pages of e-mail postings to the Zero Income Filers (ZIF) discussion group mentioned earlier (SUSAO-00703 through SUSA0-01313).

14. To the best of my recollection, all 650 pages of postings were from January of 2001.

15. Another set of discovery items which the Government disclosed to me on September 9, 2003 were copies of one hundred forty-eight (148) pages of e-mail messages (SUSAO-010650 through SUSA0-010798) which I had posted to the Zero Income Filers (ZIF), Tax-FreedomNow (TFN), and Investigating Curious Evidence (ICE) Internet discussion groups.

16. My belief is that I am not being prosecuted because of my income tax activities; I am being prosecuted for exposing Israel's and others loyal to Israel's involvement in the September 11, 2001 terrorist attacks against the United States.

17. For approximately the last twenty-five (25) years, Irwin A. Schiff of Las Vegas, Nevada has been challenging the legality of the federal income tax laws, advising Americans that anyone can legally stop paying federal income taxes, and encouraging anyone who would listen to him to "legally" stop paying federal income taxes using his procedures and methods.

18. Mr. Schiff has been conducting these activities through books he has written, e.g., *How Anyone Can Stop Paying Income Taxes* (1982); *The Great Income Tax Hoax* (1985); and *The Federal Mafia: How It Illegally Imposes and Unlawfully Collects Income Taxes* (1990); through his well-publicized political campaign in 1995 and 1996 to become President of the United States as the candidate from the Libertarian Party in the 1996 Presidential election; through his Internet Web site www.paynoincometax.com (Pay No Income Tax.com); through his business, Freedom Books, located at 444 East Sahara Avenue, in Las Vegas, Nevada; through his radio talk show in Las Vegas, Nevada, which was also broadcast over short-wave radio, by satellite, and over the Internet; through countless income tax seminars he has conducted all over the United States; through video-tapes and audio-tapes of his seminars; through audio-tape updates to the books he has written (the Schiff Audio Reports); through extensive commercial advertising he has purchased; and through numerous television, radio, newspaper, and magazine interviews he has granted.

19. For many years the Government did very little to attempt to enjoin Schiff from promoting his income tax theories and from encouraging Americans to "legally" stop paying federal income taxes.

20. On April 6, 1995 (shortly after Schiff moved to Las Vegas, Nevada), Special Agents of the Internal Revenue Service (I.R.S.) confronted Schiff in his automobile. Schiff resisted the I.R.S. agents' attempt to confiscate his vehicle and he was pepper-sprayed and arrested. However, the I.R.S. subsequently dropped any charges it had filed against Schiff.

21. To my knowledge, the only other time (until relatively recently) that the I.R.S. had attempted to force Schiff to comply with the internal revenue laws was on August 11, 1999, when Schiff was summoned to produce his books and records at an I.R.S. audit at the I.R.S. offices in Las Vegas, Nevada. After nearly two hours of interaction between Schiff and the I.R.S. agents who were attempting to audit him, Schiff refused to produce his books and records and no further action was taken by the I.R.S. or the Justice Department against Schiff. Schiff subsequently included an audio recording of this audit interview in his Schiff Audio Reports, Series 6, Tapes 1 and 2. He used it as an example to his followers of how to handle an I.R.S. audit and to prove to them that the I.R.S. has no authority to audit a person's books and records and that nothing would happen to them if they refused to produce their books and records.

22. In its civil action against Schiff, the Government was only attempting to collect federal income taxes, penalties and interest from Schiff for tax years 1979 through 1985, inclusive! The Government took no other legal action to attempt to collect taxes from Schiff for any other tax years, nor did it attempt to enjoin Schiff from promoting his income tax theories and from encouraging others to challenge the legality of the federal income tax laws. Furthermore, the Government has not prosecuted Schiff for his income

tax-related activities. For many years Schiff touted the Government's inaction against him as proof that his assertions about the federal income tax being entirely voluntary were correct.

23. To my knowledge, the Government has only recently attempted to enjoin Schiff from promoting his income tax theories and it has yet to prosecute Schiff for obvious violations of the internal revenue laws.

24. To my knowledge the Government has not prosecuted any other Schiff followers other than myself, or if it has, it has only prosecuted a very small number of them.

25. As further proof that the Government was aware of Irwin Schiff and his income tax activities, on May 15, 2003, the Government disclosed to me two hundred eighteen (218) pages of court cases involving or mentioning Irwin Schiff. These cases are Bates stamped numbered from SUSA0-00169 through SUSAO-003 87.

26. On January 15, 2003, I wrote letters to Government officials about my concern that certain Government employees were purposely allowing Schiff to remain in business so that the I.R.S. could collect more money in taxes, penalties, and interest than it would otherwise be able to collect and for other reasons.

27. The next day, I also e-mailed a copy of the letter I sent to President Bush to much of the national and local news media. The e-mail I issued was entitled "Open Letter Regarding Justice Department and Internal Revenue Service Malfeasance."

28. Schiff published his latest book, The Federal Mafia, thirteen years ago and he has over 400,000 of his books informing Americans that they can legally stop paying federal income taxes in circulation.

29. I believe that the decision to selectively and vindictively prosecute me either originated with the Justice Department in Washington, D.C. or with some person or persons higher up in the Bush Administration.

30. I believe that the Assistant Attorney General for the Criminal Division of the U.S. Department of Justice, Michael Chertoff, is Jewish and a dual-loyalist to both the United States and Israel.

31. In 2002 former Louisiana state congressman and former U.S. Presidential candidate David Duke authored a book entitled "Jewish Supremacism."

32. Former German and former Canadian citizen, Ernst Zundel (who is well-known because he raises questions regarding certain facets of the Holocaust), was arrested at his home in Tennessee by the U.S. Government and deported to Canada, even though he is legally married to an American citizen.

33. Once I realized that I was being vindictively and selectively prosecuted by the U.S. Government for alleging that Israel and those, loyal to Israel were responsible of the September 11, 2001 terrorist attacks against the United States and that I intended to vigorously defend myself in this Court by filing this motion, I realized that my life might be in danger because these interests are extremely powerful and they permeate nearly every facet of our society.

34. So I wrote letters to the President of the United States, the Attorney General of the United States and many other officials expressing my concerns for my life in the hope of circumventing any attacks against me by these extremely powerful interests.

35. As another method of attempting to circumvent any retaliation against me, I also e-mailed my concerns

and a copy of my letter to President Bush to as many media outlets as I could think of.

36. I understand that any false statements made in this affidavit will subject me to the penalties of perjury.

Steven A. Swan

Sworn and subscribed before me on the 14th day of October, 2003.

CHRISTINE M. BOURGEOIS, Notary Public

My Commission Expires March 22, 2005"

Not surprisingly, Judge Barbadoro denied my motion, as he had done with virtually all of the motions I filed. However, by getting this issue officially on the court's record, I could now raise it on appeal in the event that I was convicted.

In writing this book, I realized that the primary emphasis of my motion to dismiss was because I was being unlawfully prosecuted to prevent me from continuing to widely disseminate my belief that Zionists had orchestrated 9/11 as a False Flag operation against their enemies in the Middle East, Muslims. However, I neglected to emphasize that I might also be being unlawfully prosecuted to prevent me from continuing to widely disseminate the derogatory information about the actions of Israeli Jews provided by Dr. William Pierce and by Fox News. In any event, I do not believe that it would have mattered. Judge Barbadoro probably would have denied my motion anyway.

After I filed this latest motion, I widely distributed press releases to numerous various entities about it. I also wrote a letter to the Attorney General of the United States asking him to investigate my allegation that I was being vindictively and selectively prosecuted by the Government. I then widely distributed press releases about my request to him.

At this point, I knew that I would need even more time to prepare to defend myself against my prosecution by the Government. So I filed a motion for yet another continuance. It was granted. The new date for the commencement of my trial was February 3, 2004. At that time, Judge Barbadoro ruled that I would not be granted any more continuances.

After I filed my motion asking Judge Barbadoro to dismiss the charges against me because I was being vindictively and selectively prosecuted by the Government after widely disseminating evidence detrimental to powerful Zionists in Israel and in the United States, my Jewish standby counsel, Attorney Shklar, asked Judge Barbadoro to allow him to withdraw as my standby counsel. He said that he could not be associated with someone so rabidly anti-Semitic as I was. (Is not it interesting that if someone criticizes a Jew whatsoever, he or she is automatically labeled "anti-Semitic"? Quite often, he or she is also labeled a "racist." That begs the question, is Judaism a religion or a race?)

But how could he label me "anti-Semitic" after I had spent the past five years or so of my life doing everything that I could think of to try to disseminate Jew Irwin Schiff's federal income tax beliefs to as many individuals as I could? So I contacted Attorney Shklar and informed that I was not anti-Semitic; I simply was attempting to expose what some ruthless, murdering, corrupt Zionists had perpetrated against the United States and its citizens. After I explained my position to him, he withdrew his request to cease being my standby counsel.

The Government Had to Prove that I Had Intended to Violate the Law

One of the elements necessary for the jury to convict me on most of the charges I was facing was that I had intended to violate the law. Since I had not intended to violate the law, I tried to think of ways in which I could prove that fact to the jury. I figured that I could get sworn statements from my income tax clients, seminar attendees, radio talk-show hosts who had interviewed me numerous times, etc. and submit them as evidence. I informed Judge Barbadoro of my intent.

Assistant U.S. Attorney Morse then filed a motion with the court asking it to preclude me from presenting that type of evidence at trial. Judge Barbadoro ruled that he was going to allow me to present just about anything I wanted to present regarding whether or not I had intended to violate the law. I issued a press release regarding Judge Barbadoro's ruling and received quite a bit of media coverage about it.

I Increased Disseminating My Belief Regarding 9/11

Once I realized that I might be being prosecuted by the Justice Department, not for my income tax activities over the previous five years, but rather to try to prevent me from continuing to disseminate derogatory and incriminating information about powerful Zionists, I decided to increase my disseminations even more! I went to the local Public Access cable television station and learned how to produce my own weekly television show!

The population of Manchester, New Hampshire was approximately 100,000 people at that time. Add to that figure the populations of all of the contiguous towns sharing the same Public Access TV channel and it probably was approximately 150,000. That was quite a few people to try to disseminate my message to.

The name of my weekly Public Access cable TV program was *New World Order Watch*. In it I informed people about a cabal of the wealthiest, most powerful people in the world who facilitated the usurpation of the system of governance and commerce our forefathers instituted subsequent to the American Revolution. That cabal is comprised of many of the world's elected leaders (including a number of U.S. Senators and Congressmen and representatives of the U.S. President), the heads of multinational corporations, much of the First World's royalty, academicians, labor leaders, executives of global news and entertainment media, etc. (Individuals such as these are called "oligarchs" or "plutocrats.") Because of the power they wield, they are able to control most of the information we receive.

They name of that group of oligarchs/plutocrats is the "Bilderberg Group." They have been meeting as a group ever since 1954 when they met at the Bilderberg Hotel in Baden-Baden, Germany. Each of the United States presidents since at least Gerald Ford has been controlled by them, except for Ronald Reagan. Jimmy Carter was even president of the Trilateral Commission, a sister organization, before becoming President of the United States. In 1980, Ronald Reagan did not want long-time Bilderberg Group member, George H. W. Bush as his running mate. However, Reagan was virtually forced by extenuating circumstances into taking him. It did not matter much, though, since many of Reagan's advisors and cabinet heads were Bilderberg Group members.

During my TV show, I also disseminated information about a separate, powerful group of individuals who have control of most of the world's news and entertainment conglomerates. They are a group of powerful Jewish Zionists. (At the time that my home/office was raided by the I.R.S. in 2002, the majority of the global news and entertainment conglomerates were controlled by Jews. Even Rupert Murdock, the head of News Corporation, is half-Jewish.) Even though these two groups (the Bilderberg Group and certain powerful Jews) are separate entities, many of their interests (e.g., looking out for their own best interests rather than the interests of society as a whole) overlap. I do not know if there are any power struggles between these two groups of power elites.

I do not remember how many different weekly episodes of *New World Order Watch* I produced in the Fall of 2003 and the Winter of 2004 and I do not have that information at hand as I write this. I think that I produced approximately ten (10) of them. In addition to producing my weekly cable television show *New World Order Watch*, I also launched a website entitled "9-11 Cover-Up." It was located at 9-11coverup.com.

Chapter 6. My Trial

Prior to my trial commencing, the Government was late in providing me with a number of disclosures it was required to give me. So the commencement of my trial was moved back another three days to February 6, 2004 to make up for it. However, jury selection was still scheduled to commence on February 3rd.

Also prior to my trial commencing, the Government filed a motion in limine with the court. A motion in limine requests that the judge issue an order limiting the scope of something that the party's adversary was intending to do. This motion in limine was for the judge to force me to exclude improper legal arguments and irrelevant evidence at trial. (There are many legal arguments with respect to federal income taxes that have previously been overruled by the courts. The Government did not want be to make any of them and risk the jurors becoming confused and not accepting the Government's legal arguments.) However on January 29, 2004, Judge Barbadoro denied the Government's motion.

On January 30, 2004, my Final Pre-Trial Hearing was held among the prosecutors, Judge Barbadoro, and myself. I agreed to stipulate to (agree to) a number of facts of the case regarding my activities during the almost five years I spent disseminating Irwin Schiff's federal income tax revelations. Me stipulating to those facts meant that the prosecutors would not have to waste time trying to prove them to the jury. Also at that hearing, the prosecutors and the judge asked me if I wished to reconsider my decision to make the Government prove that I had committed the crimes with which I was being charged and plead "guilty." I told them that I was not going to plead "guilty" to crimes I had not committed, even if it meant a more lenient punishment for me if I were to be convicted.

One of the elements of most of the charges against me that the Government had to prove was that I did not really believe what I had been espousing about federal income taxes for the past almost five years. However, I really did believe what I had been espousing. One of the ways I could have tried to convince the jury that I really believed it would have been for me to call some of my clients and seminar attendees as witnesses. I could have asked them if I had ever given them any indication whatsoever that I did not truly believe what I had been espousing. However, I was reluctant to do that because I was afraid that the I.R.S. or the Justice Department might retaliate against them by auditing them or indicting them. So I did not call any of them.

Over the years, I had also been interviewed quite a few times by a couple of radio talk-show hosts in the Manchester, New Hampshire area. In fact, one talk show host, Ann Conceison, had even allowed me to host her whole program a number of times without her being present. I was going to call her and fellow radio talk-show host Woody Woodland to testify on my behalf, but I decided against it. Again, I was concerned that the Government might retaliate against them for doing so. My decision to not ask any of these witnesses to testify on my behalf probably weakened the strength of my defense.

One of the things that a defendant in a criminal case is allowed to do is submit a set of instructions to the judge for him to give to the jury prior to trial (jury instructions). On February 3, 2004, I submitted my proposed Jury Instructions to Judge Barbadoro.

Also on February 3rd, Judge Barbadoro, the prosecutors, and I also began selecting a panel of twelve (12) jurors and two (2) alternate juror to sit in judgment of me during my trial. There was one juror who I allowed to be dismissed from having to serve who, in hindsight, I wish I had kept.

I did a tremendous amount of my legal research in preparation of defending myself at a law library adjacent to the New Hampshire Supreme Court in Concord, New Hampshire. The head librarian there was very helpful to me. By coincidence, her husband was one of my potential jurors. He asked to be dismissed from having to serve because he had followed some of my income tax activities and some of my pre-trial activities that had been in news reports. He was not sure that he could be completely unbiased if he were to be a juror in my case. In hindsight, I wish that I had kept him on the jury. He probably could have been fairer, more unbiased, and less intimidated by the prosecutors than the rest of the jurors.

My Trial Received Very Little Media Coverage

My case was commonly referred to as a "tax protestor" case. Usually federal tax protestor trials attract a substantial amount of attention from the local and sometimes national news media. However, my case was given very little news media coverage. Why? Because I widely disseminated that I felt that I was being prosecuted by the Justice Department, not for my income tax activities, but, rather, to silence me from further disseminating derogatory and incriminating information about Zionists—their criminal activity within the United States, their spying upon the United States, my belief that they had orchestrated 9/11 as a false flag operation against their enemies in the Middle East (Muslims and Arabs) in order to dupe the United States into greatly increasing its military presence there and waging war on its enemies, etc.! I had even gone so far as to produce a cable television show in which I disseminated my beliefs and made my allegations!

My Trial

On February 6, 2004, my trial commenced. It began with Opening Statements, first by the Government and then by me. The Government then began presenting its case to the jury. A portion of the Government's prosecution included calling as witnesses some of the individuals named in my indictment for whom I had prepared Zero Income Tax Returns. After the Government finished "examining" them, I got to cross-examine them. I asked each one of them if they were ever aware of me saying or doing anything which would have led them to believe that I did not truly believe what I had told them about federal income taxes. Each one of them stated that they were not.

Over the years, the courts have established novel methods of ensuring that the Government succeeds in winning most of the charges that it brings against criminal defendants. It makes new case law to suit its own needs. Then other judges are free to use that new case law when issuing their own legal opinions. Contrary to popular opinion, judicial opinions are not based as much upon Constitutional or statutory mandates as they are upon prior judicial opinions, *i.e.,* prior case law.

The argument that the Justice Department used with the jury to try to overcome my defense that I was not guilty because I truly believed what I had been espousing for so long was that I had engaged in "Willful Blindness." That is, that I knew what the law actually stated and that I "willfully blinded" myself to that law. However, it was not true that I willfully blinded myself to the law; I really believed what Schiff had been espousing for so many years and of what he had been convincing many thousands of other American.

After approximately four days of the Government prosecuting me, it was my turn to present my defense. The way that a person examines him- or herself when a *pro se* litigant is to just present his or her case to the jury. The judge asks "what would you like to tell the jury?" After the person is finished with one item, the judge asks "now what would you like to tell the jury?" That goes on and on until you are finished presenting your case. That is called "Direct Examination."

Then the prosecutors get to cross-examine you. After they are through, you get to finish with anything else you would like to say. That is called "Re-Direct Examination." My Standby Counsel, Attorney Shklar, assisted me with things like the presentation of my exhibits to the jury

I had thought of playing a three (3)-hour videotape to the jury of my mentor, Irwin Schiff, conducting one of his income tax seminars. That way they could have seen for themselves how persuasive, convincing and dynamic a speaker he was. They could have seen for themselves how he was able to convince me and many thousands of other American that there was no law making the federal income tax mandatory and that no one was legally required to pay it.

Or I could have presented to them select passages of his latest book, *The Federal Mafia: How It Illegally Imposes and Unlawfully Collects Income Taxes."* Perhaps they could empathize with him as I had as he recounted how he believed that he had been railroaded into federal prison in the 1980s for challenging the legality of income taxes.

Instead, I opted to play for the jury my own two (2)-hour videotape of me presenting a federal income tax seminar. I thought that they would surely be able to ascertain that I truly believed in what I had been espousing for almost five years and that, therefore, they should find me "not guilty."

After a six (6)-day trial. It was time for Closing Arguments. The Government went first and then it was my turn. Unfortunately, I had a very bad common cold that day. I was sniffling a lot and wiping my eyes a lot. I should have explained to the jurors that I had a bad cold, but for some inexplicable reason, I did not. In hindsight, the jurors probably thought that I was crying! That was not a good impression for me to make. They must have thought that I was crying because I was guilty!

The jury deliberated for a couple of hours. Just before they came back into the courtroom, I asked Assistant U.S. Attorney Morse if it was too late for me to accept the Government's plea offer! He said that it was good to see that I still had a sense of humor.

The jury came back into the courtroom and rendered its decision. They found me "guilty" on all eighteen (18) felony counts! I was not really surprised that they had convicted me on Count 1—Interfering with the Due Administration of the Internal Revenue Laws, but I was surprised that they convicted me of all of the other counts. As soon as clerk read that the jurors had found me "guilty" on Count 2, I knew that I was going to be convicted on all of the counts! I then asked the clerk to "Poll" the jurors to try to ensure that none of them had been coerced into convicting me, which she did. None of them changed their votes.

The judge dismissed the jurors, scheduled my sentencing for May 19, 2004, and allowed me to remain free on Personal Recognizance bail. He also gave me one (1) week to decide if I wished to have my standby counsel, Attorney Shklar, represent me at my sentencing hearing, have another attorney represent me, or represent myself.

He informed me that I was not allowed for have a standby counsel for sentencing. He then adjourned the court.

There was hardly anyone present in support of me on my side of the courtroom. However, the Government's side was packed! I think that the U.S. Attorney shut down his whole office so that they could all watch the professional prosecutors (one specially brought in from the Tax Division of the Justice Department in Washington, DC) defeat a lowly *pro se* tax protestor litigant such as myself.

Before Assistant U.S. Attorney Morse left the prosecution's table, I heard him say that he hoped that his next prosecution was an easy, hand-to-hand, drug-sale case. That was rather than the "paper case" that I had just made him endure. I had filed numerous pre-trial motions in my case (to each of which he had to write a response) and I had raised numerous issues at trial. I estimate that it must have cost the Government at least a couple of hundred thousand dollars to prosecute me! Perhaps they will think twice before they selectively and vindictively prosecute someone again to prevent them from exposing corrupt special interests. Naw, I doubt it. It's not their money!

In hindsight, I should have kept my courtroom defense as short and as simple as possible. I should have explained to the jurors as if they were children that for each of the counts against me, there were certain elements that the prosecutors had to prove. I should have delineated each element and highlighted the ones that the prosecutors failed to prove. I should have then told the jurors that, because the prosecutors had failed to prove those elements, the jurors had no choice but to acquit me.

In addition, I do not think that I should have made all of the jurors sit through my two-hour video seminar. All they wanted to do was get this trial over with so that they could get back to their lives. The same thing happened in the O. J. Simpson murder trial in the 1990s. Those jurors were sequestered for nine (9) whole months before they reached a verdict! They did not care if they found Simpson "guilty" or "not guilty." All they wanted to do was reach <u>some</u> agreement so that they could finally return home to their families and their lives. Being sequestered for nine months must have felt to those jurors like they were the ones in prison!

The Erwin Rommel School of Law had counseled me not to even try to win at trial because the judges are so corrupt that they will do anything and everything that they can to ensure that the Government wins. They said to just get as many issues on the record as possible, as well as any mistakes that the judge and the prosecutors might make. However, I think that I came close to being acquitted. If only I had conducted my defense a little differently.

The Government rarely loses a federal criminal trial. One of the reasons for that is because many of the jurors are spellbound by the whole process. The jury selection and the trials themselves take place in beautiful federal courthouses adorned with lots of beautiful wood, stone, and metal work, as well as art work. The judges sit above everyone wearing long, flowing black robes. The professional prosecutors are all nicely dressed, well-mannered, and articulate. All kinds of purported "evidence" against the defendant is visible within the courtroom. And the prosecutors and their witnesses will lie through their teeth about anything and everything and the judges allow them to get away with it!

What chance does a common citizen have of winning when the odds against him or her are stacked like that? The Government rarely loses a federal criminal trial in one of its own courthouses and with one of its own employees presiding over it!

My Motion for Judgments of Acquittal

On occasion, juries make mistakes in convicting a criminal defendant. In those instances, a defendant can ask the judge to overrule the jury's verdict. That is called seeking a judgment of acquittal. After I was convicted, I filed a Motion for Judgments of Acquittal with Judge Barbadoro on the basis that the Government had not proven that I did not really believe what I had been espousing all those years. In other words, it had not proven that I had willfully violated the law. Not surprisingly, Judge Barbadoro denied my motion.

Preparing for My Sentencing Hearing

After a federal criminal defendant has been convicted of committing a crime, the federal court's Probation Department begins preparing a Presentence Report and Recommendation to assist the judge with his or her sentencing of the defendant. It is a lengthy process in which the defendant is interviewed and an investigation into his or her background is conducted. Family, friends, business associates, etc. can be interviewed and they can also submit letters in support of the defendant. The Government officials who investigated the defendant in the first place are also interviewed.

On April 16, 2004, a little more than two months after I was convicted, I received a copy of the U.S. Probation Department's Presentence Report and Recommendation for me. It was quite a lengthy report which contained quite a few mistakes and misrepresentations from the people that they interviewed. In it, the U.S. Probation Department recommended to the judge that, under the Federal Sentencing Guidelines, I be sentenced to between 11.25 years and 14 years in prison and that I be fined between $17,500 and $175,000 for the eighteen (18) felonies for which I had been convicted!

Most other people probably would have been shocked at such a recommendation. However, I was not really that concerned because I believed that I would be able to either have my convictions overturned on appeal or have whatever sentence the judge imposed on me reduced on appeal.

I knew that it would take quite a while for me to prepare and submit my objections to the many mistakes and misrepresentations contained in the Presentence Report and Recommendation. So I filed a motion with Judge Barbadoro asking for an extra thirty (30) days to submit those recommendations and a continuance of sixty (60) days for my sentencing hearing. The judge partially granted my request by approving my thirty (30) day request and rescheduling my sentencing hearing to June 24, 2004.

On May 11, 2004, I informed the court that I had decided to represent myself at sentencing rather than ask Judge Barbadoro to appoint my standby counsel to represent me. Shortly thereafter, I wrote a letter to the federal Clerk of Court asking him to discontinue sending copies of court notices to my former standby counsel. On June 4, 2004, I received a letter from the Chief Deputy Clerk of Court advising me that standby counsels remain as such until the conclusion of the case. That information directly contradicted what Judge Barbadoro had told me on the day of my conviction! (Another mistake by Judge Barbadoro!)

On June 14, 2004, I filed a motion with the court requesting that Judge Barbadoro recuse himself from sentencing me for bias against me because he had denied the majority of motions I had filed in this case. Not surprisingly, he denied that motion as well.

While I was awaiting sentencing, I received no less that three (3) letters from Assistant U.S. Attorney Morse advising me that under the rules, I was required to pay an assessment of $1800.00 to the court at my sentencing hearing. That was $100 for each of my eighteen (18) convictions. AUSA Morse knew that I was indigent, but, apparently he enjoyed harassing me.

My Sentencing Hearing

On June 24, 2004, I attended my sentencing hearing at the U.S. District Court in Concord, New Hampshire. I ultimately discovered that the basis for my sentence was going to be the amount of money that I had caused the U.S. Government to "lose" during my courses of conduct for which I had been convicted.

As I stated previously, Schiff and his many followers did file federal tax returns with the I.R.S. each year. However, we stated on those returns that we owed no tax for a variety of reasons, e.g., that we had no income tax "liability" because there was no law making anyone "liable" for the tax and that we had no "income" based upon the legal definition of that term according to Schiff's research. We included with each tax return a two- to three-page attachment delineating our positions.

In addition, since be believed that we did not owe any federal income taxes, we also requested refunds of any money that had been withheld from our pay or that we had paid to the I.R.S. voluntarily in Estimated Payments. However, very few individuals ever received any refunds from the I.R.S. Once in a while someone did, but not very many, though.

Under the Federal Sentencing Guidelines, if an individual requests a refund from the Government to which he or she is not entitled, whether he or she ever received it or not, it is considered to be a loss to the Government! So the Government looked through all of the tax returns I had prepared for other individuals and for myself during the years that I did so. Then it totaled all of those requested refunds in order to determine how much money I had caused the Government to "lose." All tolled, that figure came to $3.3 million!

So Judge Barbadoro used that figure to determine how long of a prison sentence I should receive. He looked up $3.3 million loss on his chart and it revealed that my sentence must be at least 108 months! That equals 9 years! He told me that he believed that my sentence should only be five to six years, but that there was nothing that he could do about it because the Federal Sentencing Guidelines are mandatory. As a judge, he had no discretion to change my sentence. (I remember a number of years before this, a federal judge in New Hampshire had quit his job after the Federal Sentencing Guidelines had been put into effect. He stated that since he no longer had any judicial discretion, a chimpanzee could do his job!)

I was also sentenced to one year of Supervised Release upon the completion of my prison sentence. During Supervised Release, inmates are under the direct supervision of a federal probation officers. If they violate any of the restrictions imposed upon them, they can be reincarcerated if the infraction is severe enough.

Assistant U.S. Attorney Morse also pressured Judge Barbadoro to impose a monetary penalty on me. He and the probation officer were arguing about what that amount should be. However, Judge Barbadoro, knowing that I did not have any money, said that he was not going to impose any monetary penalty upon me!

Judge Barbadoro then ordered me to surrender myself to the U.S. Marshal's Office in Concord, New Hampshire on July 9, 2004 to begin my term of incarceration. At that time, I thought that the closest minimum security, federal prison camp to New Hampshire was in Pennsylvania. So I asked Judge Barbadoro to recommend to the Federal Bureau of Prisons that I be incarcerated there. He said that he would take it under advisement.

I was not really all that concerned that I had just been sentenced to serve nine (9) years in federal prison. That was because I felt that I had raised enough appealable issues during the pre-trial and trial phases of my case to get my sentence greatly reduced or overturned. Moreover, I had learned some other tactics from the Erwin Rommel School of Law to use to try to get my sentence reduced or overturned in conjunction with the appealable issues I had raised.

Blakely v. Washington

The day after my sentencing, my standby counsel, Attorney Shklar, telephoned me and informed me that on the same day that I was sentenced, the Supreme Court of the United States issued a ruling in a case involving state sentencing guidelines that they were unconstitutional because they used information other than the facts determined by a jury to sentence a defendant. (State and Federal Sentencing Guidelines do not rely upon facts determined by juries to sentence those convicted of crimes.) That case was *Blakely v. Washington*, 542 U.S. 296 (2004). And since most state sentencing guidelines were modeled after the federal sentencing guidelines, it seemed like it would only be a matter of time before the federal sentencing guidelines would also be deemed "unconstitutional." So Attorney Shklar advise me to draft a motion to Judge Barbadoro asking him to vacate the sentence he had imposed upon me because it was also probably unconstitutional and then resentence me. So I did.

However, before I could file my motion, I received a telephone call from one of the court clerks advising me that Judge Barbadoro had unilaterally decided to vacate the verbal Judgment he had imposed upon me because of *Blakely* and schedule me to be resentenced on July 21, 2004.

Objection to the Presentence Report and Recommendation

On July 1, 2004, I spoke with legal brief writer Theo Kamisinski about my situation. (He was the legal expert who had advised me to get a Federal Defender to represent me after I was raided by the I.R.S.) He advised me to file a formal objection to the Probation Office's Presentence Report and Recommendation since much of it no longer applied in light of upon the Supreme Court's recent landmark ruling in *Blakely*. He told me that he would prepare it for me.

On July 19th, I received the Preliminary Objection to the Government's Sentencing Memorandum that Theo Kamisinski had prepared for me. It was twenty (20) pages long. The Appendix to it was four hundred (400) pages long! It also contained a request to continue my sentencing because many federal courts were in turmoil subsequent to the *Blakely* decision and also because I only was given three days to review the Government's Sentencing Memorandum post *Blakely*.

The objection also stated that since none of the determinations made by the jury were used to sentence me and only determinations made by Judge Barbadoro were used, my sentence should only be from zero (0) to six (6) months. I filed it with the clerk of court the next day.

My Resentencing Hearing

On July 21, 2004, I attended my Resentencing Hearing. My request to have it continued had not been granted. During the hearing, Judge Barbadoro deemed the Federal Sentencing Guidelines unconstitutional based upon the Supreme Court's decision in *Blakely*. He was then free to resentence me using other criteria.

Judge Barbadoro then stated that even though he had opined during the course of my original sentencing hearing that he believed that I should only be sentenced to five to six years of incarceration, upon further reflection he felt that a six-year sentence was appropriate in my case. So he sentenced me to six years of incarceration! He also sentence me to one year of Supervised Release upon the completion of my prison sentence. He then ordered me to surrender myself to the U.S. Marshal's Office on August 4, 2004 to begin my incarceration.

On August 3, 2004, I filed a notice with the clerk of the U.S. District Court that I intended to appeal my convictions. I also requested and received a transcript of my entire six-day trial, paid for by the Government.

Chapter 7. I Began Serving My Sentence

Prior to commencing my period of incarceration on August 4, 2004, the U.S. Marshal notified me that rather than surrendering myself to him, I could surrender myself directly to the Federal Medical Center (F.M.C.) Devens in Ayer, Massachusetts. The Federal Medical Center Devens is a federal prison that includes a hospital. The former Fort Devens U.S. Army Base was torn down and a new federal prison was built around the original Army hospital.

Adjacent to F.M.C. Devens is a minimum security federal prison camp. That was where I was going to be incarcerated. So on August 4, 2004, my former girlfriend and I drove to F.M.C. Devens and I began my six-year prison sentence.

After I self-surrendered to F.M.C. Devens, I was taken to the Special Housing Unit or SHU. It is also known as "the Hole." This is where new incarcerees awaiting placement in the regular prison are held, as well as those who are being punished for some infraction of prison rules. It consists of two-man cells with an upper and lower bunk, a toilet and a sink.

Some inmates are in solitary confinement. A tray with your meal is passed to you through a slot in the door three times per day. New incarcerees are allowed to go outside into a large, fenced-in area for one (1) hour per day. However, new inmates are segregated from inmates who are being punished. Because it is a prison medical center, different classifications of inmates are incarcerated there, all the way from Minimum Security inmates to Maximum Security inmates. After I reported to F.M.C. Devens, I spent eighteen (18) days in the SHU before being placed in the minimum security "Camp."

The minimum security inmates at the Camp provide much of the labor to run the entire prison. Everyone incarcerated there must have a job. Some work in an off-site warehouse and handle the food, clothing, and other supplies for the prison; others transport those items into the prison; some work in the Camp kitchen; some mow the prison's lawns; some perform maintenance duties; some perform janitorial duties; some work in the Mail Room; etc. The pay began at 11 cents per hour.

If an inmate did not wish to eat the prison food, he could purchase packaged food items through the Commissary. On a certain day each week, inmates would submit an order. A few days later, a Commissary truck would deliver the items to the inmates. There were a couple of microwave ovens in the laundry room, so quite a bit of microwave cooking took place. Inmates could also buy sweatshirts and sweatpants, other athletic wear, and other items. The sale of merchandise to inmates is a large source of revenue for the Bureau of Prisons.

When I was not working for the prison, I spent most of my time working on the appeal of my convictions to the First Circuit Court of Appeals in Boston, Massachusetts. It was docketed as *United States v. Steven A. Swan*, No. 04-2078. I invested a lot of time and effort working on that. However, what I was really waiting for was the Supreme Court of the United States to issue are ruling such as the one it had issued in *Blakely v. Washington* regarding the State of Washington's sentencing guidelines except this ruling would deem the Federal Sentencing Guidelines unconstitutional. Then my sentence would have to be reduced to a minimum amount of "time served" and a maximum amount of six (6) months.

That decision finally came in January of 2005 when the Supreme Court issued a single ruling in two cases— *United States v. Booker,* and *United States v. Fanfan* 543 U.S. 220 (2005). However, the Supreme Court's ruling in these cases was so convoluted and so confusing that it did not really change anything! It was not a decisive ruling deeming the Federal Sentencing Guidelines unconstitutional and, therefore, null and void. Rather, it allowed my six-year sentence of incarceration to stand! So I continued working on my appeal.

I also attempted to employ some of the other tactics that I had learned from the Erwin Rommel School of Law to try to get my sentence greatly reduced or overturned. They included alleging that the judge and the U.S. Attorney in my case had conspired to engage in corrupt procedures against me. That meant that they could be sued as members of a Racketeering Influenced Corrupt Organization or R.I.C.O., which I did. I also filed Complaints for Judicial Misconduct against Judge Barbadoro and encouraged my supporters to file them as well, which many of them did. There were also a couple of other tactics that we tried. One of the purposes of all this was to get the fact that Judge Barbadoro was corrupt into his official judicial record. Another was to become such an annoyance to him that he would commute my sentence.

My Appeal

With respect to my appeal, first I had to learn a whole new set of court rules—the Federal Rules of Appellate Procedure. These are the general court rules for all of the circuit courts of appeal in the country. Plus, each individual circuit court of appeals has its own rules, so I also had to learn the Rules of the Circuit Court of Appeals for the First Circuit. The First Circuit is the appellate court for all of the U.S. district courts in the districts of Maine, New Hampshire, Massachusetts, Rhode Island, and Puerto Rico.

In the U.S. Circuit Courts of Appeals, the appellant (the person appealing some lower court's ruling) files the first Initial Brief with the court. Then the appellee files its Initial Brief in response to the appellant's brief. Then the appellant files its Reply Brief in response to the appellee's Initial Brief. Then the appeals court makes its decision. The decision is usually made by a three (3)-judge panel.

A new attorney was appointed by the U.S. Attorney for the District of New Hampshire to respond to my appeal of my convictions. He was First Assistant U.S. Attorney Peter Papps. Assistant U.S. Attorney Morse would also be assisting him.

I had raised many issues during the course of my trial in the lower court. However, I could not use all of them in my appeal. There were simply too many. So I had to choose the most important ones and the ones I felt were the most likely to result in my conviction being overturned.

The issues that I raised on appeal were:

1. That the district court erred by denying my motions for judgments of acquittal since the Government presented no evidence demonstrating that I believed that the tax returns that I had filed with the I.R.S. for myself or that I prepared for others were false, or that I corruptly endeavored to interfere with the due administration of the internal revenue laws;

2. That the district court erred by denying my requests for dismissal of the charges against me regarding the fact that I was being selectively and/or vindictively prosecuted for exercising my First Amendment rights regarding my belief as to who really perpetrated the September 11, 2001 terrorist attacks against the United States and their reasons for doing so;

3. That the district court's actions of denying my motions delineated in this brief (and others); of refusing to state its essential findings on the record so that this court would have reviewable material; of erroneously ruling that my court-appointed standby counsel would not be available to assist me with the sentencing phase of my case; etc. may reflect the court's bias in favor of the Government, or against me, or both;

4. That the district court erred by not dismissing the charges against me due to the fact that the federal income tax is not imposed in accordance with the original intent of the Sixteenth Amendment to the U.S. Constitution—a tax to be imposed solely on the earnings of the wealthy.

I finally finished my Initial Brief and filed it with the circuit court of appeals on August 31, 2005—over a year after I began my incarceration! The Government filed its Initial Brief on November 18, 2005. I then filed my Reply Brief on January 12, 2006.

On July 6, 2006, a three (3)-judge panel of the Circuit Court of Appeals for the First Circuit finally rendered its decision in my case. It upheld my conviction!

It stated that I could not use the argument that I did not agree with the income tax laws because they were unconstitutional because that argument had been overruled so many times in previous court proceedings. However, neither I, nor Schiff, nor any of Schiff's many thousands of followers ever declared that we believed that the income tax laws were unconstitutional. We believed that they were not mandatory. So the Appeals Court erred in that ruling.

With respect to my argument that I was not guilty because I truly believed what I had been espousing, i.e., I had not willfully violated the law, the court stated that I had made no showing that a reasonable jury could not have found that I knew my tax obligations and I intentionally renounced them. That ruling was completely contrary to the fact that I had provided a tremendous amount of evidence delineating that I truly believed what I had been espousing.

With respect to my claim that my convictions should be overturned because I was the victim of selective and/or vindictive prosecution by the Justice Department, the court overruled it because the investigation of my activities began before I engaged in the speech that I claimed triggered my prosecution. True, the Justice Department began investigating my income tax activities before I engaged in that speech, but it did not initiate any prosecutorial actions against me until after I had engaged in that speech. Again, the court was in error.

And with respect to my never-before-submitted-to-a-federal-appeals court claim that the federal income tax was unconstitutional because Congress had expanded it beyond the original intent of the Sixteenth Amendment, the court simply stated that there was no evidence to support that argument. It stated that even though I had submitted a tremendous amount of evidence that the original intent of the Sixteenth Amendment was to impose an income tax solely on the earnings of the wealthy. Again, the appeals court was wrong.

I then filed a motion with the court to reconsider its decision in my case. It denied my motion.

I Asked the Supreme Court to Consider My Case

The only option that I had left was to try to appeal my convictions to the Supreme Court of the United States. That is called filing a Petition for a Writ of Certiorari. However, there are a few thousand requests made each year for Supreme Court review of cases and the Supreme Court only accepts a small percentage of them. So I filed my Petition for a Writ of Certiorari with the Supreme Court anyway, but the Supreme Court declined to hear it.

The other tactics that I employed to try to get my sentence greatly reduced or overturned completely were not that effective, either. I learned that in order for them to be effective, a person would need at least a modicum of money for filing the R.I.C.O. lawsuit and the Complaints for Judicial Misconduct and in preparing Complaints for others to file. Unfortunately, at that point I did not even have a modicum of money! So there was nothing else that I could do but finish serving my sentence!

Finishing My Sentence

When inmates in the federal prison system near the ends of their sentences, they are usually then transferred to a "halfway house" to being attempting to become reacclimated to living in society once again. I left Federal Medical Center, Devens on April 28, 2009 and went to the Pharos House in Portland, Maine. It was difficult trying to find a temporary job while I was there, but I finally found one at a Wendy's fast-food restaurant in South Portland.

On September 2, 2009, I was allowed to finish my prison sentence at my mother's home under what is called "Home Confinement." I had to wear an electronic monitoring device on my ankle while I was there. I could not leave my mother's home without receiving prior permission to do so. The reason that I went to my mother's home was because I had no money, no place to live; no job, no car, no girlfriend or wife, nothing. Thankfully, my mother was kind enough to take me in. Otherwise, I would have been living on the street somewhere!

October 23, 2009 was the last day of my prison sentence. Because I was given credit for my "Good Behavior" while incarcerated, my six-year sentence only lasted approximately five years and two and a half months. I met with my probation officer in Portland, Maine that day and the electronic monitoring device was removed from my ankle.

At that point, my one-year sentence of Supervised Release began. During that time, I had to stay out of trouble, seek employment, make monthly reports to my probation officer, etc. That period formally concluded on October 22, 2010. I was a free man, again (although a man with nineteen [19] federal felonies on his record! In addition to the eighteen [18] income tax felonies for which I had been convicted, I also had a conviction for possession of cocaine from way back in 1983)!

Chapter 8. Conclusion

Here is a summary of the major events that occurred in my case:

- 1995 I met nationally-known income tax protestor Irwin Schiff when he was in New Hampshire campaigning to become the Libertarian Party candidate in the 1996 Presidential election. He espoused that there was no law making the federal income tax mandatory and that anyone could legally stop paying it.
- 1996 After Schiff convinced me that his income tax revelations were true, I decided to stop paying federal income taxes myself.
- 1997 The I.R.S. put my small real estate agency in Auburn, New Hampshire out of business.
- 1997 I was so convinced that Schiff was correct and that it was the federal government that was violating the law that I decided to do everything I could think of to try to disseminate Schiff's revelations to as many other Americans as possible. I engaged in that endeavor for almost five (5) years.
- September 11, 2001 Terrorists committed lethal attacks against the United States of America.
- September through December, 2001 I widely distributed my belief that Zionists had orchestrated the 9/11 attacks as a False Flag operation in which they blamed the attacks on their enemies in the Middle East (Muslims and Arabs) in order to dupe the United States into greatly expanding its military presence in the Middle East and waging war on the Zionist's enemies. I also widely distributed evidence damaging to the Zionists about their spying activities against the United States, their involvement in organized crime and drug smuggling in the United States, etc.

- January 9, 2002 Armed I.R.S. Special Agents raided my home/office and the Justice Department informed me that I was the target of federal criminal investigation into violations of the internal revenue laws.

- March 7, 2003 I was indicted by a federal grand jury on eighteen (18) counts of felony violations of the internal revenue laws.

- February 2004 I was tried and convicted in U.S. District Court in Concord, New Hampshire on all eighteen counts.

- June 24, 2004 I was sentenced to nine (9) years of incarceration to be followed by one (1) year of supervised release.

- July 21, 2004 My sentenced was reduced to six (6) years of incarceration to be followed by one (1) year of supervised release.

- August 4, 2004 I began my federal prison sentence at the Federal Medical Center, Devens in Ayer, Massachusetts.

- August 31, 2005 I began appealing my convictions to the Circuit Court of Appeals for the First Circuit in Boston, Massachusetts.

- July 6, 2006, a three (3)-judge panel of the Circuit Court of Appeals for the First Circuit denied my appeal and upheld my convictions.

- 2006 I asked the Supreme Court of the United States to review the circuit court of appeals' denial of the appeal of my conviction. The Supreme Court refused.

- I finished my term of incarceration on October 23, 2009. I finished my term of supervised release on October 22, 2010.

Evidence That I Was Targeted by the Justice Department

Below is some of the evidence upon which I am relying for my belief that I was targeted for criminal prosecution by the Justice Department in an attempt to prevent me from continuing to widely disseminate extremely damaging information about Zionists:

- Some of the extremely powerful Zionists who I believed were dual loyalists to both the United States and Israel and who were employed by the United States when I was raided by the I.R.S. were Director of the C.I.A. George Tenet; Deputy Secretary of Defense Paul Wolfowitz; head of the Criminal Division of the U.S. Department of Justice, Michael Chertoff; Deputy Secretary of State, Richard Armitage; 1st Assistant Secretary of Defense for Global Strategic Affairs, Richard Perle; National Security Council operative, Elliott Abrams; White House Press Secretary for President George W. Bush, Ari Fleischer; one of the Pentagon's Defense Policy Board members, Kenneth Adelman; one of President Bush's speechwriters, David Frum; and head of the Defense Department's Office of Special Plans, Douglas Feith. (Michael Chertoff later went on to become the Secretary of Homeland Security under President George W. Bush.)

- Powerful Zionist dual loyalists in the media at that time I was raided by the I.R.S. were co-founder of *The Weekly Standard* magazine, William Kristol; political commentator and columnist, Charles Krauthammer, *Wall Street Journal* editor and columnist, Max Boot, and many, many more.

- The brother of Douglas Feith, the head of the Defense Department's Office of Special Plans, was the head of the criminal division of the New Hampshire U.S. Attorney's Office, the very office which was prosecuting me! His name is Donald Feith. (Douglas Feith and the Office of Special Plans were also instrumental in the United States' invasion of Iraq based upon flawed information.)

- Usually when the Justice Department decides to prosecute someone criminally, they charge as many co-defendants as possible and attempt to get them to testify against each other in exchange for less severe sentences for themselves. They begin with lesser figures to an enterprise and then work their way to the top. In contrast, I did not have any co-defendants indicted along with me.

- I was the only one of Irwin Schiff's many thousands of followers who was targeted. Schiff himself was not even targeted! Life went on as usual for Schiff and his followers. (Schiff and a couple of his associates were eventually prosecuted a couple of years later, but to wait so long was highly unusual.)

- Since I was living and conducting my income tax activities in New Hampshire and my mentor, Irwin Schiff, was living and conducting his income activities in Nevada, one would think that the U.S. Attorneys for each of those districts would be working together in prosecuting us. Instead, the U.S. Attorney in New Hampshire was working alone to prosecute me.

- I think that one of the reasons that Schiff was even prosecuted at all was because I complained so much about me being the only one of his many followers to be prosecuted. If I had not complained so much, Schiff may never have been prosecuted at all! (In hindsight, I wish that I had not complained so much and that Schiff had never been prosecuted. That would give even more credence to my assertion that I was selectively and/or vindictively prosecuted to prevent me from widely disseminating my beliefs and other information detrimental to Zionists.)

I will leave it up to you to decide whether or not you agree with my belief that I was targeted for criminal prosecution by the Justice Department in an attempt to prevent me from continuing to widely disseminate extremely damaging information about Zionists.

If anyone has any definitive factual evidence that I was deliberately targeted for criminal prosecution by U.S. Department of Justice officials because of what I widely disseminated about 9/11 and/or Israeli spying and Israeli criminal activity within the United States, please share it with me. I can be reached at contact@RailroadedorNot.com. Thank you.

www.ingramcontent.com/pod-product-compliance
Lightning Source LLC
Chambersburg PA
CBHW061308110426
42742CB00012BA/2105